Taking A Part

GS Misc 608

Taking A Part

Young people's participation in the Church

David Green and Maxine Green

The National Society
*Leading Education
with a Christian Purpose*
Church House Publishing

The National Society/Church House Publishing,
Church House,
Great Smith Street,
London SW1P 3NZ

ISBN 0 7151 4939 3

Published 2000 by the National Society and Church House Publishing
on behalf of the Board of Education of the Church of England.

Printed in England by Halstan & Co. Ltd

Contents

Foreword

Many people believe that a powerful indicator of a thriving and vibrant Church is one in which there are young people and children actively involved. Some congregations feel disturbed and daunted that they do not attract more people, or lament when children in the Church leave in their early teens.

In *Taking A Part*, young people from all over England share what has worked for them and offer their thoughts and ideas. These might be used in all churches to turn 'disenchanted youth' into active contributing church members. The authors also explore the culture of the Church and give the reader ways of explaining what is happening in their own situations and how to bring about change.

The Board of Education hopes that this book will help those in parishes and dioceses who actively want to encourage young people to offer their gifts and skills to their churches and communities.

✠ Alan Blackburn
Chairman, Church of England Board of Education

List of contributors

The authors wish to thank the following people who have contributed to this volume by allowing their quotations to be used:

Jennie Bigg, Stephen Dunham, Stuart Emmason, Paul Fawcett, Phil Green, Angela Gough, Naomi Hall, Karligh Hamblin, Tracey Hemmerdinger, Tim Hirst, Xanthe Holliday, John Hookway, Javed Kamruddin, Katie Knowles, Heather Maclachlan, Lucas Meagor, Paul Niemic, Stephen Palmer, Michael Palin, Mike Pilavachi, Sue Pinnington, Stephanie Rawlings, Philip Taylor, Ronan Wade, Ruth Ward, Emma Watson, Rob Wickham, Jacqs Williams, Andy Winmill, Andrew Whitehead.

Acknowledgements

The authors wish to thank a number of colleagues for their encouragement and support in the process of putting this book together:

Pat Barton, Janice Overington and Peter Ball of the National Youth Office, and Gill Montia and other colleagues at St Albans Diocesan Youth Service for much practical as well as moral support.

Chandu Christian and our Diocesan Youth Officer friends for inspiration and support.

Our families have not been untouched by work on this book. Thanks to our partners, Chris and Ann, for putting up with conversations dominated by *Taking A Part* and to our offspring, Ben and Zelma, Ben and Tim, for the insights and opportunities over the years to put some of our thinking into practice!

1

Introduction

A letter from a young clergyman gave suggestions for the title of this book –

- *We're Human Too*
- *Screaming against the Wind*
- *Lost in the Crowd*

When *Youth A Part* was presented to the General Synod in 1996 a small group of young people from the Southwell Diocese put on a performance at a fringe meeting to show what it felt like to be young and in the Church. It was shocking when they came into the room wearing papier mâché masks. One mask had a hand across the mouth, another a foot on the head, another a hand over an eye, another a fist in the mouth and the last was a plain, sad face. There was an enormous sense of relief when they took off their masks and offered the rest of us an upbeat message about us all being part of the Church.

This is where this book starts, with the energy of young people who are not being heard, and feel as if their heads are being stamped on. Young people who do not feel that they are being treated as human beings, are screaming against the wind and are lost in the crowd. These voices are not low mutters, they are screams to the organization of the Church, screams that we, the adult Church, are filtering out and blocking.

The other voice crying to be heard is from all of us within the Church who are acutely aware of the Church's increasing irrelevance to the wider society, especially to younger people in that society. However relevant we as Christians may think Christianity is, to most people in Britain today religion has no meaning and the inside of a church is a very foreign place. For this to change we need different ideas, thoughts and directions. A potential group who could source this new strategy is young people, and this book aims to explore ways in which this is happening already within the churches and how the wider Church can learn from this and change.

This is not the first mention of the importance of young people participating in the whole of the Church. Youth A Part, the report on young
people in the Church which was published in 1996, includes a broad
vision statement drawing the report together that reads:

> The vision is for a Church that takes young people seriously. It is a
> Church where young people fully and actively participate at every
> level. It is a Church that is built on good relationships, where young
> people particularly are concerned, not only with each other, but with
> those inside and outside the Church. It is a Church where there is a
> good theological understanding of why and how it goes about its
> work with young people. It is a Church which recognizes that work
> of this quality needs resources and has the faith and courage to com-
> mit significant resources to the young people in the Church.
>
> (Youth A Part, 1996, p. 161.)

This vision statement is not just for young people but for all people in
the Church. It was further endorsed and focused by General Synod in
July 2000, when a resolution was passed commending young people's
participation (see Appendix 2). We would hope that all people regardless of age would be taken seriously and participate in church life in
ways that would help them to grow as well as build up the community
of which the church is part. The principles in this book are relevant for
all ages. However, young people are a marginalized group. They are
often **apart** from the Church rather than **a part** of the Church. The figures in Youth A Part and in subsequent smaller-scale research show a
steady decline of young people in the Church. When we have talked to
young people they say that much of the worship is irrelevant to their
needs, they do not find ways of expressing faith and meaning within
Church and they find Church structures unhelpful, even alienating. This
is why this book focuses on young people – but why participation?

When 'young people' come under discussion within parishes there is a
tendency to think of them as a passive group who need ministering to
or a problem group who need managing. The thought that the young
people might be able to help others in the Church in real and dynamic
ways is rarely considered. Almost all adult solutions are seen in terms
of the growth and development of young people, and the thought that

they might be able to bring a different perspective to the wider Church decisions is not in the frame at all.

In my work as a Diocesan Youth Officer, I tend to find the concern for young people expressed in three ways:

- the need to do something in relation to young people who are currently part of the Church because of a fear that they will leave;

- the fear of what will happen to the Church with few young people now to become adults in the Church of the future;

- the need to reach young people outside the Church in ways that are culturally relevant.

It is our experience that where young people play an active role in the life of a church there is growth, not only of the young people but also of the church. To paraphrase J. F. Kennedy, 'Ask not what you can do for young people, ask what young people can do for you.' If we could manage to do this flip in perception and see young people as not only a resource but as a **necessary** resource for the Church it would revolutionize relationships. We would not need to look at the issue of participation in a dry way, we would be fervently trying to engage young people in ways which made sense, fitted in with their commitments, priorities and lifestyles, and valued and sought their contributions.

When we spoke to young people who were engaged with church life, a key feature was that they were involved, they had a role and responsibilities: in short they were participating fully and actively.

I would like to describe something of the transition I felt between being just a 'normal' part of the church, and being really involved. Before I did my year out, I was not the most outgoing person in the world, and I thought that my place in the church was three pews from the back. I was an active member of youth groups and music groups, etc., but as a young person I felt like I was inferior and that my experiences and ideas were all very well, but that I would have to accept that it was an adults' church which adults ran, for other adults and children, but not for young people. My year out came along at the time when all my friends dropped out of church, through going to uni, or just through lack of interest. It was difficult at first to be on my own, but then I realized something. People (adults) had started asking me to come and lead sessions at their youth groups – visual and music workshops, youth weekends, worship planning sessions. It seemed like I was now accepted and respected. Part of it is of course, the fact that I was approaching adulthood, but I think a big part of it was my own attitude about my own skills. I never thought I was particularly good at anything I might be asked to do, but as soon as other people started telling me that I had gifts and that I should use them, I could actually start to believe it. I still don't think I'm fantastic at anything that I do, but I have so much confidence that I would do it anyway, whether it's leading a congregation in singing, serving on a committee, or saying what I think when the bishop asks me.

I think basically, what I'm saying is that young people not only need encouragement and praise, they also need opportunities to use their skills and to build their confidence.

Andrew Whitehead, Young Adult Network.

The Church is not alone in addressing the subject of participation. The Government are looking at ways of consulting with children and young people. At local authority level councils are setting up young people's forums and gatherings. The youth service has always seen the 'club committee' as a powerful agent in enabling young people to develop and shape both themselves and their club. It seems that wherever you look someone is discovering the potentially powerful contribution young people have to offer and the need for them to be 'on side' rather than detached and disaffected with our organizations and institutions.

In this book we are also able to draw on theological reasons why young people need to be truly a part of the Church. Saint Paul's picture of the people of Christ as a body (1 Corinthians 12.12-31), shows that each part is necessary for the proper functioning of the whole body. This offers us a powerful challenge if we are choosing **not** to use the gifts and skills of the significant group of young people in the Church. His attention was not focused on the part of the body that is not being used and feels undervalued but on how the rest of the body is incapacitated without an eye, or a foot.

As we were writing the book the parable of the talents (Matthew 25.14-30, *Good News Bible*) became a powerful point of reflection when we consider the story and how it can relate to young people:

At that time the Kingdom of heaven will be like this. Once there was a man who was about to go on a journey; he called his servants and put them in charge of his property. He gave to each one according to his ability: to one he gave five thousand gold coins, to another he gave two thousand, and to another he gave one thousand. Then he left on his journey. The servant who had received five thousand coins went at once and invested his money and earned another five thousand. In the same way the servant who had received two thousand coins earned another two thousand. But the servant who had received one thousand coins went off, dug a hole in the ground and hid his master's money.

After a long time the master of those servants came back and settled accounts with them. The servant who had received five thousand coins came in and handed over another five thousand. 'You gave me five thousand coins, sir,' he said. 'Look! Here are another five thousand that I have earned.' 'Well done, you good and faithful servant!' said his master. 'You have been faithful in managing small amounts, so I will put you in charge of large amounts. Come in and share my happiness!'

Then the servant who had been given two thousand coins came in and said, 'You gave me two thousand coins, sir. Look! Here are another two thousand that I have earned.' 'Well done, you good and faithful servant!' said his master. 'You have been faithful in managing small amounts so I will put you in charge of large amounts. Come on in and share my happiness.'

Then the servant who had received one thousand coins came in and said, 'Sir, I know you are a hard man; you reap harvests where you did not sow, and gather crops where you did not scatter seed. I was afraid, so I went off and hid your money in the ground. Look! Here is what belongs to you.'

> 'You bad and lazy servant!' his master said. 'You knew, did you, that I reap harvests where I did not sow, and gather crops where I did not scatter seed? Well, then, you should have deposited my money in the bank, and I would have received it all back with interest when I returned. Now, take the money away from him and give it to the one who has ten thousand coins. For every person who has something, even more will be given, and he will have more than enough; but the person who has nothing, even the little he has will be taken away from him. As for this useless servant – throw him outside in the darkness; there he will cry and grind his teeth.'

The story of the talents is picked up in the main chapters in the book. We were particularly taken with the way the master chose different amounts for different servants; how he praised both the successful servants equally and asked them to 'come in and share my happiness'; how the successful servants had their talents developed by the master and so were entrusted to greater responsibilities; how the third servant was afraid and did nothing and even the little he had was taken away from him. Although it is not appropriate to parallel one situation too closely with the parable, if the servants are seen as the adult Church and the talents are the young people, it is imperative that we adopt the behaviour of the wise servants. We are being called to act prudently and wisely rather than be paralyzed into doing nothing through fear and guilt.

In this book we move through using this parable as a central thread. It is interwoven with theories relating to participation that we hope people will be able to use in their own situations. We draw on work from people writing from a sociological angle, such as White, Brew and Lake, as well as theological thinkers such as Paulo Freire. Our aim is to integrate these two features with many voices of young people and those working with them in the field. These are people who have experienced good things through participation, are highlighting difficulties they have encountered and are raising ideas and presenting new models for the future.

As always when attempting a subject as wide as this, there will be areas which we have not been able to include. Had we set ourselves the task of writing a definitive work it would probably have been a much thicker, heavier tome and would have taken several years to collate and publish. Our aim in writing this book is to share some key models, experience and practice with those who are 'doing participation' or want to do it. We are hoping to stimulate debate and discussion and to bring a resource and encouragement to enable more young people to become actively involved in their churches and in their communities. The book places a key emphasis on young people *within* the churches who are managing to be actively engaged, are hanging on in 'survivor' mode, or who are just about to drop away from the Church. These groups offer a great source of information and enlightenment to the policy makers in the Church, both in terms of how they can best be involved and how best to contact and engage with their friends and peers outside the Church. By concentrating on this primarily, we have not been able to include the many examples known to us where young people have used their own faith, vocation and calling to work *outside* the churches in their schools, colleges, work places and community. Finally, there seem to be some key challenges that became apparent to us when we reflected on the issues raised in the book and these are outlined in the conclusion.

The titles of books always come with a story and *Taking A Part* is obviously rooted in the energy and enthusiasm of *Youth A Part*. When we started, our working title was 'Taking Part'. As we have moved forward with this book it has become obvious that as well as hoping that more and more young people will be able to **take a part** in their churches and communities we will need to take some things **apart** to allow space for change. If the Church does not take the risk of loosening up existing structures and practice so that new growth can take place, there can be no change and we may as well resign ourselves to extinction.

2

What are young people saying?

I first met Simon when he was about 16 years old. He was part of the church youth group in a village near Norwich involved in planning an annual event called Grapevine. In the following years he joined the main planning group, chaired the planning group, took photographs for me for a special project and was part of the group that reviewed the Diocesan Youth Service, sitting alongside a bishop, and other key adults from various parts of the Church. At the same time others were inviting him to be involved in a range of projects. Some time later he went on to Bible College, blaming me and the Director of Norwich Youth for Christ for his move towards working in the Church.

The years have slipped by and I am now in St Albans Diocese. Last year I received a phone call from Simon, now married to Gill, 'I'm coming to plague you; we've been appointed as youth workers for a church in your diocese.' It was a real joy to stand in that church recently, speaking as part of a youth-led service and reflecting on Simon's journey and now seeing the fruit of what, ten years earlier, were just sparks and beginnings of gifts. That is the privilege of working with young people, but one which we rarely see in full as young people move away and we have to trust that the gifts we have encouraged are growing.

In the parable of the talents we read:

> . . . he called his servants and put them in charge of his property. He gave to each one according to his ability . . .

Matthew 25.14b-15a (GNB).

As we reflect on what is behind *Taking A Part* it becomes evident that participation and gifts are bound together. This parable acknowledges that we have different abilities. The master makes no value judgement in his distribution of money, rather it is based upon his knowledge of the servants. He knows their skills because of his relationship with them. Therefore giving five thousand to the first servant is not saying he is superior to the others, it is about his ability and the expectations of the master. This passage is an example where each person is given a significant opportunity for the development of his or her gifts.

Sarah (13) had never been to church at all and though she was a bright, intelligent girl she was underachieving at school. She was loud and disruptive. This was probably to do with the insecure home background that she came from. She was invited to take part in a photography project for young women, organized by a church youth worker. When she got there she found that they were talking about something she had never heard of, stations of the cross. As she liked the youth worker she decided she would stick around. The youth worker talked about prayer and about producing stations that were relevant to the young women. Eventually, having learned the skills needed, Sarah along with several other young women, went out into the area where she lived taking photographs to produce stations of the cross. The stations produced by the young women were put up in a local church alongside the rather 'chocolate box' stations that were already present. The stations were used during Lent by the church congregation and Sarah, with the other young women, began to go to these prayers and to take part, producing their own prayers.

Ruth Ward, former Diocesan Youth Officer for Southwark Diocese.

In this chapter we will explore how the culture of the Church works, the models that we carry and how these affect the way we provide and respond to opportunities for growth.

Clashing cultures

We have to face it, we, the Church, are struggling to build bridges between the culture of the Church and where many people are today. Spirituality is on the agenda of many, Church is not. In the Church, as in all walks of life we have the legacy of our history. This has many aspects to it including the way denominations have formed, emerging out of other churches and the various structures of organization that we have. One way of responding is to perpetuate a culture whose time is past, which we hang on to when threatened. Change is resisted even more strongly and we adopt a siege mentality. The result is an organization in decline. An alternative way of responding is to reflect on the culture in relation to the rest of society and, being confident of those things that make up the gospel, we become vulnerable but open to the possibility of change.

This issue is crucial and is sharpened up when we consider specific areas of work with young people, for example, the frustration of a youth worker encouraging young people to grow in their gifts and take on responsibility, only to have to stand on the sidelines of the 'adult' church until they are old enough (whose perception?) to be responsible and use their gifts. In the meantime, what do young people do? They go somewhere where they are valued and allowed to develop, which may not be Church in any shape or form. Many disengage from the Church altogether whilst for some it will be to the growing phenomenon of youth worship, youth congregations, youth churches that are growing alongside mainline Church. Many adults see this as being outside the Church, yet it is a place where gifts are recognized and encouraged, real Church for many young people. Viewed from 'main Church' it is seen as something that will pass, yet how do we know? We must avoid the assumption that the culture based on tradition and the values of adults, which is most dominant in the Church, is right and that we have nothing to learn from younger people.

The Church of England, and other denominations too, are hierarchical structures and this is reflected in the culture that we inherit. In a hierarchy it is convenient, and in a way comfortable, for one part to blame those above for the way things are. In the Church this might be called 'clergy bashing'! In practice a culture is mutually held by those within it; in the Church both clergy and laity exist within a safe culture where power is dripped downwards.

For the laity we can blame bishops and priests for holding on to power rather than releasing people to use their gifts more fully. It also saves us from having to take so much responsibility for what does or does not happen. Clergy have been known to express frustration at laity who do not seem able to make decisions without reference to them, whilst at the same time seeming to get some enjoyment from being the centre of life in a parish. This is the real stuff of being within the culture.

One way of understanding this which has been very helpful for us is using Transactional Analysis (T. A.). Although this sounds a bit daunting the model is easy to grasp and throws light on what is happening between older and younger people in the Church. T.A. says that there are three different ways we can respond to any situation, that correspond to three 'ego-states' or aspects of ourselves. We can respond from our parent ego-state, our adult ego-state or our child ego-state and these are represented in the diagram as three circles on top of each other. When anyone speaks to or approaches another person they can 'choose' which ego-state to use, e.g., 'What time do you call this?' said in a brusque voice, is a statement from person A's parent ego-state addressing the child ego-state of person B (Diagram 1). If Person A were to use their child ego-state they might sidle up to person B and say in a whiny voice, 'Have you got the time, please?' (Diagram 2). However A starts the conversation, it is up to B how to respond. In the diagram below B has chosen to respond from their 'child' to A's 'parent'.

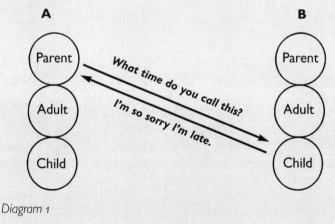

Diagram 1

Diagram 2

In any organization a culture develops and there are accepted ways in which different people behave. The Church is no exception to this and there is a distinct pattern of how we conduct our conversations and relationships. In the hierarchy, many relationships are conducted from the parent ego-state of the person higher (H in the hierarchy), to the child-state of the one lower (L in the hierarchy). Because this is the culture, L in turn responds using their 'child' and addressing H's parent. As we are so used to this, we are scarcely aware of its happening and a culture is created where the person 'above' us acts like a parent and in turn we parent those below us in the hierarchy. We can represent this chain of parenting in the diagram below.

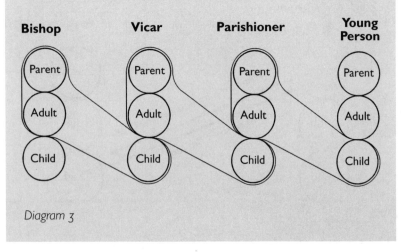

Diagram 3

There are benefits of living with a culture where we all know where we stand and where we are comfortable. The person in the higher parent role can feel responsible and powerful and the person in the child role can feel cared for and protected. However, there are also limitations to this cultural system. The first is that in any interaction between two people where they are only using part of themselves, the interaction is more impoverished than one where people could engage totally. People get frustrated – those in the 'higher' role because people leave all the responsibility to them – 'I can't believe how the members of my church are bank managers, headteachers and captains of industry but when they walk through the door they leave their brains outside.' Also those in the 'lower' role know they have ideas, thoughts and vision for their church which are never allowed to see the light of day. 'I've been worshipping at the church for two years and have never been asked what I could offer, or how my skills that I use at work might help the life of the church.' Particular 'losers' in this system are those at the end of the chain who are destined only ever to use their child ego state. It is remarkable what transformation occurs when comments to children and young people are addressed to their 'adult' ego-state.

Structures have, over the years, been created that are more about management of the institution than the activity for which it was established. A model of dependency has been established with which many of us are comfortable, while at the same time frustration is felt at all levels of the structure. However, people live with it because they have power over others lower down that structure. The real frustration and powerlessness felt at the bottom comes from a sense and recognition that all one can do is respond from the 'child' and either appeal to the 'adult' or react to the 'parent' – a factor as to why young people are labelled as 'problems' which other members of the church seek to solve by being better 'parents'.

The dependency model as illustrated above, of which we are a part, has pros and cons. It provides structure for the Church to operate within. It gives security as everyone knows his or her place. The negative elements however, in our view, outweigh the positive. Too many people reject the role of 'dependent children' and now regard the Church as irrelevant and uncaring. In a society where spirituality is so high on the agenda, church does not seem to be a place which people see as linked to their own spiritual needs. New and different styles of ministry are not easily adopted as part of the structure. People are not encouraged to be participators.

> Friendship and support are the greatest aids in the participation process. Many young people feel alienated by the Church, and they see her as irrelevant. By the simple matter of recognizing young people not as a problem, but as people made in the image of God, who are filled with the Holy Spirit, and as eager to tell others about the gospel with an urgency not found in most others, the trust of the young people may be gained. Most don't feel at home in the church environment. That saddens and frightens me – it is not the young people that need to adapt, it is the hearts of many others who attend.
>
> Fr Rob Wickham, Diocese of London.

> You can't have passion when you're being passive! I think there has to be some dynamic. If you're receiving you need to give out too, but also when you go to give you end up receiving.
>
> Andy Winmill, Diocese of St Albans.

Adolescence is a time of changes, and often rebellion is an acknowledged element, but we compound this by the approach we take. We need to challenge the basis on which the whole Church operates, to see true participation. That doesn't mean to destroy what exists, rather for each person to consider his or her use of power – either by sharing it as a wide resource for the benefit of the whole, and in doing so releasing many people, or by holding it to themselves. If we want to see real moves, it will take commitment at all levels of the Church to change from a dependent to a mutual community model.

It is the tradition of a lively evangelical/charismatic church to pray for the children and young people at the point they go into the various groups during a morning service. Depending on who is leading the service there are two different ways that children and young people are prayed for, reflecting two different theological standpoints, and thus models of participation. The first is where prayer is offered for the 'children' (this includes young people) as they go into their groups, praying for the teachers for wisdom and that the 'children' will learn more about God. The second is praying for children, young people and leaders as they go to their groups, asking that God will guide them and they will learn together new things and draw closer to God through their time together.

It is fascinating to listen to just what is prayed. In one it is about passing on knowledge with the assumption that children and young people are the only learners – empty containers to be filled with knowledge. In the second it is about sharing in the learning together, open to the possibility that God can speak through all ages. From this example we can see just how our words reflect our thinking, our theology, and its impact upon our expectations. What messages are we giving to young people through what we say in our routine words and actions?

We often hear that young people do not engage with what is going on in church. One Sunday, in the church described above, as a protest at not being acknowledged, the teenagers did not move. It was fortunate that the curate realized what was happening and invited the young people to 'go to their groups'. Was this just a silly act of rebellion, or a significant challenge to the theology and thinking of the church leaders?

Young people want to take part

Young people don't participate enough. They give the impression that they are far too apathetic. Which in a lot of cases is wrong. They simply are not encouraged and supported enough by the elders of the church to take part.

Karligh Hamblin, Diocese of Exeter.

The motivation of young people to be part of the Church is a significant element in our thinking. We begin by reflecting on some work done in the context of youth work across the country and relate this to the models of youth work that we use.

In November 1990 at a Ministerial Conference on the Youth Service, a Statement of Purpose was put forward which is regarded by the National Youth Agency (NYA), and noted in Phillips and Skinner (1994) as the most widely accepted current definition of youth work, with its broad statement:

> The purpose of youth work is to redress all forms of inequality and to ensure equality of opportunity for all young people to fulfil their potential as empowered individuals, members of groups and communities and to support young people during their transition to adulthood.

It then continues by identifying four areas which, when taken together, set youth work apart from other forms of education. These are couched in terms of offering opportunities which are educative, designed to promote equality of opportunity, participative and empowering. Under participative it states:

> Participative – through a voluntary relationship with young people in which young people are partners in the learning process and decision-making structures which affect their own and other young people's lives and their environment.

Earlier, the Review Group on the Youth Service in England (1982, p. 32) found, in their discussion with young people, a strong desire to be involved, to have their views respected and heard. They found young people wanted to have a real say in decisions that affected their welfare and refuted the claims that giving young people the authority to make decisions did not work. There was instead the feeling that those in positions of power and influence, whilst claiming to believe in the right for participation, were sometimes unwilling to accept the implications when decisions were made.

It is significant that the Statement of Purpose outlined above, never received ministerial backing. In spite of this, it has been widely accepted and used by many local authorities and agencies working with young people. It seems that for the Government, participation and choice are related to individuality and a consumer-supplier relationship. Unfortunately, there is still a movement within church youth work to follow a model where the youth workers provide a programme of activities for the young people to take part in, as consumers. One of the ways this approach has been challenged is through the emerging development of cell groups. These are peer-led groups where young people are encouraged to take responsibility for themselves.

I lead a cell. It works because there's not just one figurehead for it, my job is to help other guys to realize their potential, find out what their gifts are and help them develop these gifts. It's also to build up a community thing where we work for each other and, most importantly, draw closer to God.

I was brought up in a conservative evangelical church, I've been a Christian since I was three but hadn't really experienced much of the Holy Spirit. I joined a pioneer cell group through Sound Nation in St Albans and found out what worshipping God really meant. Through that I discovered what my gifts were; now I lead worship and write songs and so on. Leadership – I've always had leadership abilities but it gave me the chance to find what it really means to use my gifts to glorify God.

Andy Winmill, Diocese of St Albans.

I'm old enough to have escaped from the label of 'He's still in full-time education so we'll treat him like a schoolchild'. St Botolph's as a church sees the older end of the youth as a valuable leadership resource (there are several others besides me). Age appears to be irrelevant, in that if you have a talent or a gift in some area that can be of use to the church, then you are encouraged to use those gifts – age is not a significant issue. **It is through this willingness to take young people of all ages seriously that a Sunday congregation of about 60 can muster youth groups with a combined attendance to match it!** From serving on the PCC I find my opinions being listened to. Friends suggesting changes to the operation of an established choir have been listened to. Members of a youth group asking questions or struggling with getting to know God have been listened to. Basically, the church needs to listen to its young people, teach, rebuke and correct in Christ's love where necessary, and encourage the young to participate and have a voice.

Stephen Dunham, Diocese of St Albans.

The buck has to stop somewhere

There seems to be consensus that young people should grow into 'responsible adults', whatever that might mean. If we are actually to achieve this, adolescence must be about more than their being controlled. Young people need to prepare for adulthood, and the best context is within the community.

The complexity of this issue comes to the fore in the question of balancing control and empowerment. It is easy to assume all control is negative and all empowerment is positive, but experience tells us this is not so. Earlier we reflected on how our words and actions tell others what motivates us. In this context it is important to know where we stand, because we will be exposed by our actions.

It is at this point of acknowledging that someone is held responsible that theory and practice are revealed. A significant factor is how we, as adult members of the Church, perceive young people. In *Children in the Way*, the model put forward was that of all ages together on the pilgrim path, at different stages of the journey, yet there to support and encourage each other on the way. The essence of this concept is that whatever our age, status or wellbeing we are all equal in God's eyes as pilgrims. Refugees, on the other hand, are people without homes, without status and without power. They often have strength, otherwise how would they survive? But they are driven by others towards anyone who will give them help. Do we see young people as fellow pilgrims or as refugees?

Positive empowerment, being seen as a pilgrim, is where people know the constraints and boundaries of a situation but are then given freedom and choice within those. This can start very early as children. Parents very quickly offer choices to their children. 'Would you like this or that?' As they get older more choices are given and the consequences of making those become more important. In the context of church a focus is often worship and the involvement of young people. To be given clear boundaries of what can be done and what cannot, with defined areas for input, gives real opportunity for someone to get involved. In contrast with this, to fail to offer help with music, liturgy and organization would be to disadvantage them or even set them up to fail.

> Our cell supervisor is really helpful. She's there as a safety net but is really into us having ideas and helps us develop those ideas with passion. With Marc, leading worship, I helped him and learned from him: now I'm leading worship and helping other guys. One of the good things about cells is that it is all about modelling stuff, and what I've had done for me is what I now want to do for others.
>
> Andy Winmill, Diocese of St Albans.

> The Cell café started as a social for our cell, we took over the church hall, we had loads of food out, music and whatever. We said wouldn't this be good as outreach, we invited everyone we knew, provided food and a DJ and it's been going for over a year now. The evenings are going really well, we rejigged things in September and they are building up again, we've changed the atmosphere. Whereas people said, 'If I'm not doing anything I'll go to café', now people are saying, 'Oh yeah café.' Everyone is involved in running it so they can all feel part of it. We do run it, we organize it and get things out of that. When it's gone well it's just great – and that is important to us.
>
> From a conversation with John Hookway, youth worker, and cell group leaders in Radlett, Hertfordshire.

The outcome of positive control and empowerment will be a sense of ownership by all involved, relationship developed, trust increased, even if things do not go as planned – the model is there to look at how it could be done, improvements made and the cycle moves on. The element that we often fail to recognize is the need to move forward and take on more responsibility. It is best when this is not thrust on people, but seen as a gradual process. We either load young people with too much and complain when they 'let us down', or we fail to provide development opportunities, so they become frustrated.

Before I was in cells I didn't speak to many adults on a mature level . . . I met up with a woman from my church the other day and we were talking about things in St Albans. I find I can support her and she me as well. The other day a woman of about 80 came up to me and said, 'I think you're lovely!' I think it's just because cells have been there for me to develop confidence and leadership. My perspective of people in church has changed; the adults respect me as part of the church and I've been more able to relate to them.

Emma Watson, Diocese of St Albans.

Whilst recognizing that control has a positive side to it, we must acknowledge the fact that many of us have experienced the negative aspect within our church life. The reality is that the person in the power position can withdraw their 'permit', controlling what can or can't happen. This is seen in many aspects of church life, none more so than worship.

In *Youth A Part*, a young person comments on youth worship:

Worship for young people often means that a guitar is wheeled in and a modern hymn is sung. Worship by young people means that you have to have a drama bit. (p. 63).

In our church we've begun to step back and make space for young people, like with our youth services and Sunday evening services. The congregation have seen what the young people can do, they've seen they can play a part, they've seen they can help people worship God, help people find out more about God. In our church at the moment the adults and the young people have both got to shift boundaries, both groups, however wide a range it is, can learn from the other. If Tim's sitting next to a 60-year-old who is worshipping God and being blessed and Tim's not, he can look at that person and take joy in that. Likewise, an older person might think loud music is just 'wawawa', but if Tim's getting closer to God that older person can be there saying 'great' and again take joy.

We try and encourage the fact that we all have gifts but that we sometimes have to put up with other people's ways of doing things and thank God for that as well. They've (the evening services) been really good so far and all ages are taking part and people getting involved. I relish the future and what we can do with it.

Michael Palin, Parish Youth Worker, Bricket Wood, Hertfordshire.

Valuing people

The local curate was a fan of Millwall Football Club. He found that they organized football training sessions for young men and young women on one night a week. At the youth club which he ran he asked around who would like to go. There were a number of young people who expressed an interest but explained that they had no transport. The curate organized a minibus and got involved with the training himself. Over time the relationship developed and the young people showed an interest in his church. He offered to show them around the church and explain why the objects there were important to him. Being in the Anglo-Catholic tradition there were many objects to look at. Some of the young people expressed a wish to come to church but explained that they were nervous. The curate arranged for them to come along and found jobs for them to do such as serving and welcoming. Eventually some of them were asked to do readings and to produce prayers.

Ruth Ward, former Diocesan Youth Officer for Southwark Diocese.

The importance of the positive elements of the parent role is highlighted in how young people are supported as they move towards adulthood, and struggle with gaining independence. It is interesting that young people tend to feel valued by their peers, where relationships are formed around shared values. In contrast young people, in the main, do not feel valued by adults. This is tied up with status where, if young people retain the status of children, adults can retain power and responsibility for decision-making. At the other extreme, particularly where young people express their desire for some independence, some adults will remove all their support. The reality is that young people need support and information, provided in a responsible way.

Empowerment amongst young people is on the increase, but, as I look around at these guys sitting here, compared to many other youth groups I know, they do far, far more. They take a lot more responsibility and they have grown through the responsibility.

We are thrown in the deep end, and we have to help each other. When you've had a cell when everyone has contributed you go away at the end saying that was so good. When you get people doing part of the evening word, worship, witness, welcome – it helps the structure; when everyone contributes you can learn in different ways, means you see things from different ways. We have to adapt how we do things to fit the people in the cell; everyone contributes, everyone is equal, cell leader helps that happen.

More and more people are taking responsibility, offering to do things, which is great. Some still don't like to do things, or offer, you just have to learn which ones to encourage and which ones to let offer.

From a conversation with John Hookway, youth worker, and cell group leaders in Radlett, Hertfordshire.

As with many aspects of life, we need to learn how to participate. This is done by starting small and building up progressively, for example by sharing decision-making and negotiating responsibility. As people grow in confidence and trust, the responsibilities can be renegotiated and thereby the balance of power changes.

The Faith in the Countryside (1990) Commission raised the issue of recognizing the value of young people. In listening to young people the commission found that:

> Many young people talked of lack of relevance of worship and church life to their own lives, though they appeared to retain a keen interest in the spiritual dimension. Other young adults, who may be called upon to take on responsibility and be fully involved in decision-making processes in their domestic and working lives, say that within the Church they are frequently de-skilled and excluded from leadership positions (pp. 229–30).

The Commission went on to highlight ways in which other denominations involve young people in decision-making and particularly highlights the Fellowship of United Reformed Youth (FURY) and the way in which issues are raised and fed into the systems of the Church. In the summary of recommendations they write:

> The role of young people in the on-going life of the Church should be examined to seek ways of enabling them to participate fully at all levels of Church life according to their individual skills and talents. (p. 238).

My cell is not linked into a church, so far it has been separate from my church. What cell has done is make my faith real and equip me and through it I started getting challenged about the way I was living. Cell is a safe place where you can learn and develop. Then I started to impact my church – putting back into it what I had learnt. Without cell I would probably, even now, just be going to the youth group and having a laugh there, possibly not even going to church. Now I'm at church making an impact, influencing people and showing them how it can be. It has benefited the church.

Tim Hirst, Bricket Wood.

Once they started to give us responsibility they realized we could do this, and from then on thought, 'We can give that to them to do'. It has worked; we have been given more responsibility recently.

And most of us have thrived on it as well.

More roles in church, chance to get involved.

I like the feeling when the adults come to you and need you to do something, maybe they don't know how to do something – makes you feel better as well.

One thing I have gained is, I can walk down the street and meet people, have an adult conversation with them. It is a small place so you get known, that is nice, they treat you as friends, not just as 'the younger people of the church'.

In some places you feel looked down on, you don't want to go to church if it is like that. That's why in some places people go to the youth group but not to church because they are treated differently.

I also think older members of the church are genuinely interested in what we are doing, they really do care, they want to know what is going on, want to help you.

From a conversation with a youth worker
and cell group leaders in Radlett, Hertfordshire.

How, in our various situations, do we show young people that they are valued? Do we know them well enough as individuals to recognize and encourage them to develop their skills and talents?

3

Where and how
do they say it?

One of the elements of the parable of the talents that strikes us is that the master went away. He did not stay around and keep an eye on what was going on. He showed trust in the servants as well as being clear where responsibility lay. In this chapter we look at the process of participation, in particular making space for young people to take a part.

I think one of the biggest things I've learned about participation was about a year ago at a conference, from Mike Pilavachi's teaching on Samuel. Samuel really wanted to be famous and do stuff for God and God said, 'All I want you to do is anoint David.' One of the things I learnt is that sometimes we've got to take a step back and push these guys forward. I've learnt so much from my youth group through letting them do stuff. Sometimes they do it worse than you and you think I could have done that better. But the fear is that sometimes they'd do it better than you and you'd feel redundant, left out – what's the point of being here when they can do it on their own? I think the challenge is to be a bit more gutsy and let them do it; if they muck it up, fair enough, but then they won't always muck it up because they'll want to do it better.

Michael Palin, Parish Youth Worker, Bricket Wood, Hertfordshire.

Not just young people

White (1990) states:

> It is time to break down the notion that youth work is solely about young people. It is not. It is about society as a whole, it is about youth workers, and it is about struggles, oppressions and exploitation of particular categories and classes of people. (p. 6).

The same is true within the Church. Issues which affect young people affect the whole Church community. The issues raised in this book are not just about participation of young people in the Church, rather they offer an opportunity to consider the values that we hold individually and corporately and how these impact upon the way we are as the Church.

> We aren't getting young people involved in services – reading and leading intercessions. I think that is because adults don't engage in those either; we haven't expanded our base of adults that do that. There seems to be an ideal in the congregation that people have to be very good to be able to do those things. Young people are not going to have that because they don't have the degree of confidence.
>
> Revd Sue Pinnington, formerly Peterborough Diocese.

Good decisions are made with the widest consultation and consideration. If our decision-makers are only from one age group, then any decisions are incompletely sourced. The Church needs the active involvement of young people to help make better decisions. Charles Handy highlights this in his book *The Empty Raincoat* when he talks of organizations that are 'stuck' and in decline, needing the lack of history and fresh perspective of younger members to change the culture and work better. This is something we visit in greater depth later in the book.

> I just feel that young people have a view, not just older people making the choices. It's our generation that is going to take over what is now. We should be heard as well.
>
> Stephanie Rawlings, Heacham.

> At a very simple level, Jesus commands all to be like little children, and all who take the incarnation seriously must listen to the views of the young people in their care. The Holy Spirit enables each of us to become our true selves, and any hindrance of that process must be avoided at any cost. Young people are the Church of today, not just the people of tomorrow. Such participation must be encouraged at every level.
>
> Fr Rob Wickham, Diocese of London.

We often hear it said that young people are the 'Church of tomorrow', which misses the mark completely. Even to say that young people are the Church of today and the Church leaders of tomorrow does not give full justice. We need to consider that there is only ever the Church of today, with the gifts and skills that exist at that given time. Tomorrow will then be the 'Church of today', but with some differences. In this way, we can acknowledge the emerging, developing gifts rather than thinking 'today young people are part of the Church, sometime in the future they will be leaders'. How the 'gap' between now and that time in the future is used is significant.

Dependent – empty vessels

Dependency is a complex issue, as we began to consider earlier in relation to the culture of the Church. Too often it is assumed to be a one-way relationship, particularly when viewed in terms of government/welfare policy. Too often young people are viewed as dependent, rather than having a contribution to make. Thus adults (and in this respect the Church is very guilty) act as if all that children and young people can do is receive what is given and be grateful for it.

A powerful concept to consider on this issue of dependency comes from the 'banking' concept of education, in the writing of Paulo Freire. He describes it in this way:

> Narration (with the teacher as narrator) leads the students to memorise mechanically the narrated content. Worse still, it turns them into 'containers', into receptacles to be filled by the teacher. The more completely he fills the

receptacles, the better a teacher he is. The more meekly the receptacles permit themselves to be filled, the better students they are.

Education thus becomes the act of depositing, in which the students are the depositories and the teacher the depositor. Instead of communicating, the teacher issues communiqués and 'makes deposits' which the students patiently receive, memorise and repeat. This is the 'banking' concept of education, in which the scope of action allowed to the students extends only as far as receiving, filing, and storing deposits. (pp. 45–6).

In putting forward alternative models Freire goes on to write:

Knowledge emerges only through invention and re-invention, through the restless, impatient, continuing, hopeful inquiry men pursue in the world, with the world, and with each other . . . The more students work at storing the deposits entrusted to them, the less they develop the critical consciousness which would result from their intervention in the world as transformers of the world. (p. 46).

For a humanist, Freire's challenge sounds very similar to the commission to a handful of disciples 2,000 years ago, and which the Church, at least in word, holds today.

Freire challenges us to consider the model we hold and work out in our relationships and dealings with young people. Many of us have a 'deficit model of young people', viewing them as empty and resourceless and treating them as consumers, i.e. we believe that we have the skills and knowledge to impart; young people are the passive recipients with nothing to contribute. This is a fundamental mindset that must be challenged; it is the key to whether we see people as fellow pilgrims or refugees. It is not easy, because we have to find ways of convincing everyone that young people do have skills, and are resourceful. One of the difficulties we face is that many of us in the Church do not really believe we are pilgrims ourselves. If as adults we do not feel empowered, how can we enable young people to be those things?

In a small Bedfordshire town the evening service at the parish church normally saw five old ladies in attendance and a lady non-stipendiary minister leading. They were plagued by a group of about six young people whose regular meeting place was outside the church. During these evening services the young people would shout, tap the windows, climb on the roof and generally make a nuisance of themselves. Those inside, inevitably, discussed the situation and were increasingly fearful of this group. One day someone radically suggested that they might invite them in and eventually this was agreed. The lady NSM was duly (after all she was the leader!) sent to invite them in. Initially the young people wouldn't accept because they were frightened of what might happen to them. Eventually they accepted and the two groups met. They worked out that they had in common songs that were sung at school assembly and from this grew some positive and real relationships.

Early on a handbag was stolen; the owner asked the young people if they knew about it. The group identified the culprit who was encouraged to return the bag with all its contents. Relationship and trust was growing. There is now a regular youth group in the town which came from these small beginnings. A risk was taken and it paid off.

The most striking thing about this situation is the image of two groups apart from each other and fearful of each other. It took one to overcome its fear and put out a hand. For us, in the Church, our agenda includes contact with those outside or on the edge, therefore the onus is on us to hold out a hand. It is an action with risk and for many of us one which holds uncertainty and fear. How can we challenge our own fear and the fear of those **outside** the Church so that we may come together and learn from each other? How can we challenge our fear of others **inside** the Church so that we may come together and learn from each other?

Every year in Southwark Diocese, a group of young people from Anglican Catholic parishes made a pilgrimage to the Shrine of Our Lady at Walsingham. Many of the young people involved were on the fringe of the Church but for many this was a way in to becoming more involved. The young people walked from just outside London, sleeping in church halls on the way. A daily mass was held by the group before they began walking each day. The then Diocesan Youth Officer became involved and arranged that when they arrived at Walsingham they would do workshops producing their own worship which would relate to the pilgrimage that they were continuing to make. One year, just before the vote in Synod about the Ordination of Women, the young people had as their theme, 'Conflict'. It meant that whilst organizing worship, they could take on board that there were differing views held by the adults and they could talk about ways of dealing with this particular conflict. Quite a number of young people became involved with the Church as a result of these pilgrimages.

Ruth Ward, former Diocesan Youth Officer for Southwark Diocese.

Participation energizes

I will not claim that it is easy. You need to find confidence not in your-self but God's confidence in you. I look back at my life to see how it's all been stage-managed, little events coming together to effect great changes. The main problem you may face will be being accepted as an equal because subconsciously people are likely to perceive you as someone to be talked to rather than listened to. It may take a while to change this and the key to success is belief in yourself. Also don't let people cloud your understanding with jargon, always ask what it means; nine times out of ten half the other people there have no idea either. You are unlikely to find deep spiritual fulfilment at a PCC meeting but it will help you be more in touch with your church. You will start seeing God's purpose achieved through you. The changes you make may seem small and insignificant, a notice board at the back of the church for example, but it will all add up to something remarkable.

Naomi Hall, Diocese of St Edmundsbury and Ipswich.

One of the outcomes of participation, when people feel they count, is that they are more energized. This opens up another area of question and consideration, particularly in relation to worship. One of the successful organizations working with young people and influencing churches in the UK and increasingly abroad is *Soul Survivor*. They started as a group of young adults from a charismatic church in Hertfordshire who wanted to take the gospel to young people in Watford. 'Soul Survivor Youth Church' is the result. At the same time a major summer festival of that name started and over 15,000 young people attend each year. One of the key elements is 'intimacy in worship' and it is certainly true that the young people who attend appear to be energized by the style of charismatic worship.

As we grapple with this notion that participation energizes we are faced with the question, 'Is the worship participative or are people just on an emotional high?' How do we tell? What are the ways we can see participation happening? In business jargon, what are the indicators of participation? In attending such events one is often struck by their simple nature. The model they use consists of three elements:

- worship, with songs ranging from active praise to those asking deep questions about a walk with God;

- word, normally one person addressing the congregation;

- prayer ministry, when people are invited to respond to the word and the prompting of the Holy Spirit.

For *Soul Survivor*, a model of participation seems to be somehow embedded in their values; the strong belief exists that young people are equal and have gifts to use. Young people are encouraged to 'go back and use your gifts'. The struggle comes when the local church does not know what to do with young people who believe they can make a difference. In all this there are dilemmas. Does participation mean that people can come as they are, and engage as they want to? How is participation encouraged within a situation which is so led from the front? Does the nature of participation change as the congregation gets bigger? Should young people be encouraged to 'go back and use your gifts' when for many of them their local church will not understand what they are wanting to do? From the other side, would it be better not to encourage young people to believe they can make an impact; that they can be participators? These questions challenge us to think about what the indicators are in our various situations. How will we know when participation is taking place?

There are a growing number of places attempting to offer space for people to participate at all levels, where the model is around opening ourselves and 'our' power to young people; where they are invited to participate in worship, social action, finance – the list is endless; where people are encouraged to be part of the whole, bringing themselves as active participants to the situation. It is difficult and requires persistence. It is a working relationship that does, however, value everyone's contribution.

It does push us back to the heart of the question; how can we make participation better? This gives us the clue to why we would want to measure it. We often 'know' organically whether something is working or life-giving. The value of indicators as a way of reflecting what is good and what works leads us to consider what can be changed and how we might improve it. It is not easy. When, for example, someone is praying, how do we measure participation during prayer? We need to take account of the emotions and thoughts of a person, as well as physical action. They may appear to be in an 'attitude' of prayer, for example, kneeling, but how will we get to the truth of what that person is thinking and feeling during their prayers?

There is no one answer, after all we are individuals and need to be treated as such. However, it is too easy to use this as a way of avoiding listing the indicators that we use organically all the time; the things which affect our attitude, our outlook, our view of people – as pilgrims or refugees, and the value we place on them – which in turn affects our actions towards them.

When Mark first came away with the project, he refused to be involved in anything. He would lie in bed, or hide, curled up in a sleeping bag, under the bunk beds or a table. The other members of his 'gang' told me to ignore him, saying, 'He's always like that', or 'He's got attitude.' Despite participating very little though, Mark continued to turn up and be there. Our acceptance of him as he was, and encouragement of him, one step at a time, kept him coming along to events and residential weekends. Slowly but surely, Mark began to do more and to give of himself. He would clear away his dishes when asked to do so, or try out the rock climbing (in his own time!!). The day (years on), when Mark got himself out of bed in the morning and asked what he should do to help with breakfast, not only caused my heart to leap with joy, but enabled me to reflect on the truly developmental process of participation.

Tracey Hemmerdinger, Southwark Area Youth Development Adviser.

Handling the power

In her article 'Equality and empowerment: The principles of the youth work curriculum?' (1992), Sue Cockerill writes:

> Youth work cannot achieve equality and empowerment in a society that actively works against these. The very essence of youth work process is equality and empowerment. (p. 18).

She argues that seeking to address issues of equality of opportunity by targeting individuals and groups actually further marginalizes young men and women. It is the deficit model of young people that says they are deficient, and therefore something must be done to them which will result in their having the deficiency met in order to make them 'normal'.

Kearney and Keenan (1988), in their article asking whether anyone knows what empowerment means, write:

> Young people . . . lack opportunities to make their views known, to be listened to or to influence agencies and institutions that control their lives. In short, young people lack power. If work with young people is firmly based on the value of empowerment, this means holding the beliefs that:

- young people are of equal value with adults

- young people should have as much control over their lives as adults

- young people should have as much say as adults over decisions that affect them

- young people's experiences, knowledge, skills and attitudes must be recognized as real and valid even though they may not have the breadth and depth of some adults. (p. 3).

Whilst agreeing with the essence of the above, the danger in what Kearney and Keenan argue, and the way in which similar assertions have been read and put into practice, is that it seems to promote the view that empowerment is about handing over all power from one group to another. In fact empowerment is about power-sharing and the issue is about how this is done. There are good reasons why adults retain an element of 'parent', from the Transactional Analysis model. These include:

● providing a safe environment for activities;

● clear, agreed and understood boundaries which enable learning and growth to take place;

● legal responsibilities for areas like insurance and child protection;

● experience and skills of adults to enable involvement which may be outside the experience of the young people at that stage.

It is appropriate for someone to take ultimate responsibility, and in that sense be in control. The issue is how that control is exercised. If that control means that young people are not valued, their opinions and experiences have no worth, or their input into decisions affecting their lives is not sought in an appropriate way, then it should be challenged. If that control means that there is a process whereby young people are empowered, sharing responsibility for decisions in a growing and developing way, then it is positive.

As a priest, I seek to support the young people through prayer, through listening, and through the enabling of the young to take responsibility for themselves, their activities, their attitudes, and their pilgrimage with God. All people must be enabled to participate, whether they be homeless, poverty-stricken, young or someone with a hugely affluent lifestyle. Especially in the world, where money and social standing mean power. Sadly, this is also to some extent true in the Church – this must be eradicated.

Fr Rob Wickham, Diocese of London.

Empowerment cannot be merely an individual target, it has to be focused for all. Brew (1943) presented a model over fifty years ago where he identified the youth club as a means by which people could develop the skills, knowledge and disposition necessary for citizenship:

> The club at its best creates a society of personalities with a community sense, which is the essence of good citizenship . . . We are not concerned with the making of 'good club members' or 'well-organized youth groups' but with a much wider issue, the making of good citizens. This can only be done in a society where each member is important, where each one is given a chance to contribute something to the life of the group – the leader no more and no less than the member. It is for this reason that self-government is so important in club work. If I had to give the first article of my club credo it would be 'I believe in the club committee'. (p. 12).

Whilst youth clubs no longer draw large numbers of young people, the principles espoused above are still relevant: to have places where people are challenged to use power in a way that benefits society rather than just the individual; learning to be part of the community and understanding the needs of others.

As preparation for a month long water project in Kenya with a group of young people from the East End of London, we undertook a number of participatory exercises. One of these involved cooking millet porridge with a bare minimum of equipment, and sharing the resulting meal with the group. When faced with having to obtain water from a distance and figure out how to use a trangia stove, the group complained continually, but were encouraged by the prospect of the food at the end. However, they found the results far from appetizing, and very few of the members would even taste their wares. Comments such as, 'You'll never get me eating that muck', and, 'We will be taking our own food, won't we?' dominated the weekend. When actually in Kenya, even the fussiest of eaters made an effort to try the food they were offered. Being invited to participate in a warm, welcoming community produced completely different reactions from the young people, than those in the contrived training session.

Tracey Hemmerdinger, Southwark Area Youth Development Adviser

Making way

A model developed by Lake (1986) in the late 1950s which he called 'the dynamic cycle of being', takes up the theme of linking empowerment and giving value to people. Within this model four factors make up the normal pattern of interpersonal relationships:

1.   Acceptance

2.   Sustenance

3.   Status (motivation)

4.   Achievement.

Adams (1995) describes the process as part of a relationship between a youth minister and a young person. The focus here on status and achievement is the time when the young person wants to give rather than just receive. Supporting the view that young people are not just consumers of whatever we offer them, but participants and creators in a dynamic process, she highlights the importance of creating a climate in which the opportunity for the young person to give is possible. Achievement is a great motivator for people; supporting young people to see a project through to completion is an important learning experience which gives them status and value. When something is done as part of a group, achievement is enhanced; it is the 'buzz' factor that excites and enthuses a group to go on and do even bigger things.

> Young people need opportunities to give, to contribute meaningfully to the life of their communities, to expend their selves in the service of others. Sometimes Youth Ministers need to act to help create a climate in which this is possible, and need also to be willing to receive from the young people with whom they are engaged in dynamic relationships. (Adams, p. 7).

Many of us, including youth workers, have fallen into the trap of seeing ourselves as providers. Adams recognizes the need for adults to be receivers, for the benefit of the relationship with young people.

At my home church I decided to get myself on to the PCC and I was elected a couple of years ago. I was invited to be on deanery synod and I was really chuffed that they considered me for that role. A couple of weeks after I was voted on by my church the rural dean rang to co-opt me on as a youth synod member. I was happy to say that I'd been accepted by my own church to be there.

Ronan Wade, Loddon, Norfolk.

H2O is a café run by young people for young people in the town centre of Ipswich. Everyone on the management team is between 18 and 27. The majority of staff are between 15 and 20. The head chef is 15 and he oversees the whole kitchen side of the café and is responsible for people almost three times his age!! H2O is a joint venture between Bethesda Baptist Church and Centre for Youth Ministry. They have empowered young people to provide a safe, culturally relevant environment for young people to hang out on Friday nights and to give young people the opportunity to find out more about Christianity if they wish. However, it is a two-sided project – not only are we providing this service for young people, we are also giving many other young people a chance to develop skills as they run the café.

Phil Green, Ipswich.

4

How is it heard?

As we continue to consider the process of participation we focus again on our Gospel passage. The master returns and the servants come to show what they have done with the gifts he gave them. Just as he gave according to ability, so he responds in the same way. He doesn't judge between the level of gifts, but uses the same affirming words to the two whose gifts have been used and grown. So often we affirm the more public gifts, we affirm those who are very capable. In this part of scripture we are challenged to affirm all gifts and all growth, and to identify ways of responding to what young people bring, and of offering more opportunities to develop. As the master said, 'You have been faithful in managing small amounts, I will put you in charge of large amounts.'

Consequences for the Church – we need young people

We have used many examples to illustrate the experiences of young and older people in their relationship with the Church. A number of these expose the expectation of young people to question and challenge – they don't and won't sit quietly as many of us remember doing. This highlights the very different world that our children and young people are growing up in, where they are part of an education system that encourages exploration and questioning. The accessibility of images of the world pouring into many homes through television and computer screens and access to the Internet, has already had a significant impact on lives and expectations; we are told this is to increase over the next few years.

We are interacting with young people in this context – they expect to question and they also expect their voice to have value. The difficulty is that they have not always learned how to put across their point of view; when their approach seems antagonistic and appears inflexible, our response is even more important.

In Youth A Part, Denis Tully wrote:

> There is a tendency to believe on the part of adults that young people 'know it all'. This is untrue and young people

say it's untrue. What young people say is that they have much to learn but also adults have much to learn from them . . . Young people do not want to destroy and rebuild, neither are they intent on being given everything. Rather their desire is to have an experience of the Church which is meaningful to them and to walk a pilgrim journey with either their peers and or other adults. (p. 72).

If you've got just older people you have an older view. Having younger people it gives us the chance to have a say and as people who will be in it for the next 50 years, and we've like got our say but we don't want to alienate older people, we want a united church working as one body. With us being a part then everyone can feel part of the church. Doing God's will is important to me, I want to do that and if we work together as a whole church we can respond to that and hear him together.

Ronan Wade, Loddon, Norfolk.

Our vicar wants to see children and young people more involved. If you walked into our church you can't see anything that says children and young people are involved in the church. He wants to see things up in church that show that they are involved and that we really want them.

Stephanie Rawlings, Heacham, Norfolk.

At the end of the year we had a mission called 'FUSE' where 150 young people came to Plymouth for a week of training followed by two weeks of outreach. What struck me again and again was how effective young people can be. As part of this I was involved in a week of street outreaches. The number of passers-by who stopped and commented how good it was to see young people standing up for what they believe and doing something about it. It was a great way to prove that Christianity is not dead and isn't just for old people. I spent another week involved in a holiday club at a small local church. Here a team of twelve young people worked alongside members of the local church. Comment after comment was made about how we, as young people, had taught the adults so much about children's work and sharing the gospel in a way that is real and relevant.

Phil Green, Ipswich.

As adults, we have to learn to hear the message, even if it is not presented in a way that is easy to accept. Our role as youth workers and concerned leaders is to enable that voice to be spoken in a way that it can be heard. That is about a skill to speak, valuing the person and what they have to say. The essence of youth work itself – for the benefit of the community, not just for the benefit of young people.

This is a significant issue in how we, as the whole Church, perceive young people. So often we major on young people needing us and being enabled by us, all of which is crucial stuff. However, the bottom line is that we need young people in the Church. Not to have them means we lose community, energy, and feedback from the emerging generations who are, or should be, picking up the torch alongside us. Our failure to engage means the slow decline of an ageing, dying Church.

Participation is for the benefit of both the young person and the Church, although I think I would say there is more benefit for the Church. This is because, through participation, the Church has access to more and different experiences, fresh ideas, people willing to learn, and enthusiasm. Of course all young people bring different gifts, just as their older counterparts, but I think youth also is something which brings its own benefits which the Church could use and should value.

Stephen Palmer, Young Adult Network.

We are the future of the Church, and so for the Church to survive, the current leaders should invest effort in seeing that the future leaders are well equipped. Also, there is no reason why some of the youth should not have a role in the Church now. Greater years do not mean better hearing for the word of God, or for that matter, better understanding.

Philip Taylor, Young Adult Network.

Ultimately, any participation of the young people is to the glory of God. It is he who calls, develops, shapes and uses to his glory, and this means that both the young people and the rest of the Church benefit.

Fr Rob Wickham , Diocese of London.

> The Church should listen. The young should speak loud enough for the 'hard of hearing'. The Church should be ready to act as teachers and guides when needed. The young should not expect it all to be laid out for them – if they expect to be taken seriously they should go and try out their ideas, with the support and nurture of whatever organizations are available, local or national.
>
> Stephen Dunham, Diocese of St Albans.

In Charles Handy's book *The Empty Raincoat*, he talks about a company who were celebrating the twenty-fifth year of their organization (pp. 61–2). Initially, he says, the company directors thought of commissioning a history of the first twenty-five years, but they thought that a little self-indulgent and chose instead to concentrate on the future. With Handy as a consultant they were:

> persuaded that the most fruitful way to do that would be to entrust that forward look to the brightest and best of their own people, people who might be leading the organization when those years arrived . . . They were giving these young people the responsibility for their inheritance.

Handy goes on to say that the company not only gave their young people the space to think for the future but they agreed to them presenting their thoughts, findings and recommendations (unexpurgated) to a meeting of the main customers of the company. Handy says that 'it is important that the seniors give permission and encouragement . . . it is also important that the next generation accepts their responsibility'. Handy cites this example to show how an organization can continue to be relevant and appropriate. He uses a model called the sigmoid curve (pp. 49–64). This model has been used primarily in business and sales, but has significance for the way the Church can move forward. The theory is that an organization or new project starts with energy, progresses slowly, rises and then falls. This is not limited to organizations, but is a model which can also be used for empires!

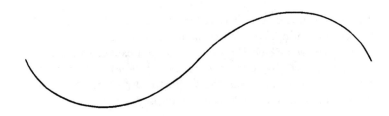

Sigmoid curve

The way a successful enterprise manages this is, when they are at the point where the curve still rises, just before they reach the top, they start a new sigmoid curve. The illustration above where the young people were invited to look at the future shows one way in which the second sigmoid curve can be started (at point A).

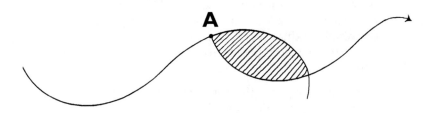

Sigmoid curves

There is an obvious lesson for the Church in this model. We have young people who are willing to give time and energy and take the responsibility for the future of the Church. It is up to the 'seniors' in the Church to give permission and encouragement.

Participation – measuring it working

From a three-week-long fund-raising café run with a large group of young people from Forest Gate, East London, we raised about £800. The young people had been involved in decorating, creating and staffing the café along with volunteers from local churches. The money went to charities chosen by the group. Both during and afterwards however, there was much talk about lost profits and 'light-fingered' volunteers amongst the group. Two years later, by popular demand we undertook the project again. This time, the young people themselves were far more involved in the developing and planning of the project. They suggested the use of cash tills, and went out of their way to put in other measures, which would avoid potential loss of profit. After another three weeks of young and old working together in the church hall, the café was this time proud to announce a profit of £2,000.

Tracey Hemmerdinger, Southwark Area Youth Development Adviser.

It is important not only to engage in the process of participation at all levels, it is also necessary to identify indicators (ways of measuring how effective the processes are) in our work with young people. The following broad-brush questions can be used as a basis for reflection and discussion about our practice:

- Does everyone have an opportunity to have an input?

- Does this involvement help increase understanding, or is it a way of people confirming their previous prejudices?

- Is there evidence of tokenism?

As a DYO I was invited to lead a PCC Awayday looking at the involvement of young people in the life of the parish. Three young people had been invited along – two young women (aged 16/17) who were on the PCC as youth representatives and one young man (aged 22) who was good at expressing his views to PCC members and the vicar. You could say he spoke loudly until people listened!

The day seemed to make good progress. We reviewed what was available for young people; we considered aspects of *Youth A Part* and how did this parish take young people seriously. On the face of it, the young people were part of a welcoming, caring church which involved them, supported them and so on. In light of this I was surprised that the young people were relatively negative and when 'collared' during lunch it became clear that they saw a big gap between what was being said and their experience. Such that, they dared not disagree with what was being said. In response to our lunchtime discussion they agreed to be put 'on the spot' and work with me to challenge the PCC.

Some swift adjustment to the afternoon programme put people into small groups (again!) but with some specific questions that had to identify actual involvement in worship, in decisions, in the life of the church. A young person was in each group and had to say what they would like to see happening in these areas.

I walked around listening to the responses, which showed where people really were coming from: 'The trouble is that young people don't understand what worship is about. When I was young we had to sit and be quiet, why can't they just do that now?' 'You are on the PCC but we don't expect you to be able to understand what goes on!'

In the final plenary, people were amazed when these things were quoted, in fact a sense of real disbelief. Yet highlighting that, in spite of apparent involvement of young people, the indicators were not about being at meetings, but about the impact their presence has in changing attitudes and understanding.

The difference between tokenism and real involvement can be seen in the positive attempts to support people to make a real contribution to a meeting which can be time-consuming.

- How do people treat the place, venue?
- Do people act as if they have a stake in the place or activity?
- Is there change taking place as a result of the activity?

A type of indication, though one that is hard to pin down, relates to the pilgrim/refugee model. If people treat you as a pilgrim, someone who is equal but possibly at a different stage of the journey, then you begin to believe you are a pilgrim. If people treat you like a refugee, someone who is homeless and without rights, always looking for someone who will help, then it is easy to live as a refugee. Therefore, to believe and hold on to the fact that in God's eyes you **are** a pilgrim, even when people try to treat you as a refugee, you act as a pilgrim. Eventually, this challenges the behaviour of others and they will begin to treat you as a pilgrim. In our Transactional Analysis model, this means working to respond from the adult ego-state, regardless of being engaged by another person's parent ego-state, until the interaction changes. It is easy to see how this can happen with individuals, though that is hard enough. To challenge a culture seems an onerous task, but is tackled one step at a time.

- Is the person growing in the things he or she does?
- Is he or she encouraging others?

When we were twelve or thirteen we were shipped off to Sunday school groups, not really given choice to stay or go. Whilst still in that group the church got refitted out and I was asked to get involved in the sound. Even though I was only 15 I was treated as someone responsible enough to get involved in this. Since then, with the cell group running, I have been given responsibility to lead something for other people.

Javed Kamruddin, Radlett, Hertfordshire.

I went with my church to Romania when I was 14; that was when I first felt God. They thought I had potential to develop leadership skills but I was quite unconfident and shy, only spoke to people I knew. When cells started in 'Sound Nation' I put my name down, I didn't really want to go, I signed up because they didn't have enough names on the list. I went and really enjoyed it, and, yeah, it helped me in a small group to be accountable. I didn't think I was going to develop leadership skills but I guess you learn, watching others lead, and develop that yourself if that is what your gifting is.

Emma Watson, St Albans.

Three young people Angeline, Karen and Mustafa were part of the Emmanuel Youth Project in an Urban Priority area of London. Through the project they grew in confidence, especially after they had taken part in the 'Water for Life' project, raising over £30,000 which they used working alongside a small village in Kenya. This experience enabled them to address a conference on development issues, where they actually made suggestions to Linda Chalker on how young people could be involved in community aid projects. Certainly the young people would never have dreamed of doing something like that before their long involvement in the Kenya project.

Tracey Hemmerdinger, Southwark Area Development Adviser.

5

Risking change

I first became actively involved in the church structure when a friend and I were invited to attend the Youth and Children's Responsibility Group as youth representatives four years ago. Initially I was very nervous but the issues they were talking about were directly affecting me and I realized that I had as much right as anybody to speak out. Two years later the same friend and I were invited to speak at a presentation on *Youth A Part* on the subject of youth participation in the Church by the DYO who had come to speak to our youth group. We knew little enough about diocesan synod, still less about the *Youth A Part* report but we knew about our experience within the Church and believed in a church owned by its members.

We even managed to face the questions afterwards from a few who believed that youth did not want to become involved in the Church. Well maybe many young people do not want to become involved in the perceived Church and in many ways I sympathize, we need to create an environment where they can believe that they can initiate change. For me it was the existence of my friend Katherine – separately we felt quite powerless but together we could make a stand. From this we have grown into confidence within ourselves. We were invited to join the Diocesan Children and Young People's Reference Group and later that year, when the future of our local youth group looked unsure, we decided to take it on ourselves. From this I have gone on to become a member of our PCC, joining a worship planning group (Sacred Space) and the Young Adult Network.

Naomi Hall, Diocese of St Edmundsbury and Ipswich.

This chapter is probably the hardest to grapple with; we are faced with the servant who buried his gift and brought to his master only what he had been given. Fear caused the servant to panic and take no action, to bury what he'd been given. The result is painful and distressing – separation from the master, in fact being thrown out. This part of the Gospel narrative seems, in our context, to be speaking to the Church and its structures. We explore issues of how the fear of failure leads us to take few risks and establish a culture where our own preferences and comfort come before anything else. We think about our perceptions of ourselves as the Church and how this affects what we do and how we do it.

What you see is what you get?

Earlier we considered the importance of how we view ourselves. Seeing ourselves as pilgrims or refugees affects how others see us, and how, over time, behaviour towards us can be changed. In the same way, perception of power is an important element of how people behave. If we believe that we are powerful in a situation then our behaviour will be different than if we see ourselves as powerless.

Considering life for young people in rural situations, Phillips and Skinner (1994) identify powerlessness, though describe it in terms of the key issues of isolation, loneliness and access. They point to the way in which young people in rural areas have little or no say in their lives. One example is the ease with which parents can influence friendships by simply denying transport (p. 36), another is the lack of affordable recreational and leisure facilities, and where they exist often having to watch holidaymakers and wealthy incomers enjoying these facilities (p. 37).

Denham and Notley (1982) identify a clear role for youth workers:

> To encourage successful participation it is necessary for youth workers to challenge positively young people's acceptance of their own powerlessness. (p. 52).

The possibility that the average person can have a real say in matters that impact upon their lives is outside many people's experience. Yet maybe this is possible within the Church. It could be the one place where people can have a real voice. However, there is clear evidence that the structure of committees and synods supports those who are most articulate and, once in position, difficult to remove. Individuals can dominate decisions over decades, thus reducing opportunity for the participation of others. This is further compounded in that when someone feels powerless the opportunity for participation reduces greatly. This in turn fuels the argument of the committed committee member that others are not interested anyway. Someone has to make the first move, and once again, the onus is on those who are in the positions of most power.

Often we see generation as a problem to participation. How can the needs of young and old be met in one place and time? For a significant number the belief is that they can't, but that is often from the assumption that there is little desire for change and growth. This story is both an encouragement and challenge:

In a parish where I worshipped some years ago lived two elderly sisters who had been born in the parish and now, in their late 80s, continued to be regular worshippers at the church. In fact they were noted for their attendance at the Family Service where few elderly folks went. In reality the 'new' vicar had turned the church around. From a congregation of a dozen, including organist and dog at the main Sunday morning service there were regularly 250 plus, including families with children of all ages.

One of the features had been the introduction of more family-friendly services which included, on occasions, the vicar playing his trumpet. After one such rendition I was talking with these two ladies and asked whether they enjoyed the new style services including trumpet. Their reply was swift, 'Oh no, it's not our cup of tea at all, but we love to see our church full.'

It seems that the very old, having lost the need to exert power, can be the wise stewards, people who are truly wanting to see the faith passed on. They are prepared to support things because they see life continuing beyond them for the church they have worked in and been part of over the years. We can learn so much from people like these; we need to celebrate them in the Church.

Mike Pilavachi, who heads up *Soul Survivor*, has also talked of the impact of 'old ladies' on the success of the work:

> Back in St Andrew's, Chorleywood, where we grew from, we realized that there was a gap between the way people wanted to worship. The teenagers loved the drums, but how can you inflict that on older folks who want a quieter approach to worship? But we are still family. The other week we invited over a group of old ladies from St Andrews who meet every week to pray for the work here. Faithfully, for seven years they have done this. It was great to have them up the front, we applauded them and blessed them for their support. They had never been here before, but they felt part of us, and we couldn't do without them.

The relationship between God and people

Relationship underpins the teaching of Jesus:

> I do not call you servants any longer, because servants do not know what their master is doing. Instead, I call you friends, because I have told you everything I have learned from my Father.
>
> John 15.15 (GNB).

The Bible has many descriptions of the relationship between God and people. We don't want to divert into an exploration of the characteristics of God, rather to note the nature of God's relationship with us. Just as any parent will adopt different styles towards her/his children depending on the situation, but will always do so from one relationship base, that is the same with God. Through the Bible we could highlight a range of ways that people have related to God, from making sacrifices and following strict regulations through to the New Testament with the graphic tearing of the curtain at the most holy place in the temple. God was now accessible to humankind. It is no longer a fear of torment and punishment, but a filial fear, out of respect and love for God.

This relationship is about partnership and participation. It is not about cowering to a despot, but sharing in the good things of the family that we, as Christians, are part of. Therefore we find that the language of equality, empowerment, choice and participation do fit into what the Church is, or should be about. These words have a strong meaning and purpose when viewed in the context of the Christian faith and the teaching of Jesus.

The Church in practice

Understanding what it means to forgive, frees people to learn from their mistakes. This in turn, frees them to use their judgment knowing that they cannot possibly always be right, but that they will be respected for having done their best.

Stamp, 1993, p.10.

Stamp offers some interesting insights into the Church from an organizational angle. She highlights the important element of forgiveness that the Church offers but identifies a 'blame culture' which has crept in and looks for who did what wrong. She contrasts this with a learning organization where the emphasis is on understanding for growth and then goes on to identify the problems of mistranslation that lead to misunderstandings. To understand forgiveness, it needs to be traced back to the classical Greek origins:

The word *hamartenein* has passed into English as 'trespass' – a word with uncomfortable, almost legalistic connotations. But its original meaning is 'to shoot and miss the mark'. (p.10).

A paper by the Methodist Association of Youth Clubs (MAYC), Manchester and Stockport District (1995), compares recent research into faith and young people. In noting the key issues from its own research document entitled *Growing Pains*, the paper states, under the heading 'Voice':

Young people feel they are unfairly blamed for damage, that adults often complain about them and that there is general lack of understanding of their needs. (p. 3).

We, the Church, need to be a place to take risks, try things out, experience freedom. So often the experience of young and old alike is to find criticism and tradition. It therefore becomes the exception rather than the rule when young people feel welcomed and appreciated. The blame culture has found its way into the heart of the Church.

Treating people as people is an area that Stamp (1992) identifies as something the Church has to offer, though it could be argued that many voluntary organizations, and in fact commercial ones too, talk of the important resource of people. She considers whether commercial and voluntary organizations are reminding the Church of key concepts that it has lost. She looks at hierarchy, empowerment and forgiveness, and notes the current position taken by management of enabling others to do their job more effectively, asking:

> Can this happen in religious organizations? It is not easy to turn a long tradition of 'standing above and overseeing' to 'sitting behind and foreseeing' especially if there is no economic imperative to do so. (p. 4).

Responding or imposing

As throughout our reflections, worship inevitably comes up as an area where many desire to respond positively to the needs of young people. Some very successful pieces of work have been undertaken, reflected in this story.

It became apparent that within the parishes in the deanery the young people, at best, were singing in choirs, serving and helping with Sunday school. They weren't actively involved in worship nor was there a good youth provision in terms of youth clubs. Paul and I brainstormed and came up with *Let RYP* – Rutland Youth Praise – a worship roadshow on a deanery basis with each parish developing its own style of worship and we bringing the kids. The deanery synod backed us, but of course couldn't give us any money. The meeting (of deanery synod) was very poorly attended, the classic problem that, 'Yes, we'd quite like young people but we don't really want to know.'

We decided to trial *Let RYP* adopting the principle that they would run the service, we provided a good key speaker – Paul, the DYO, and I set up the publicity machine. It went to every parish and all other churches. It was a disgusting, wet January night and we got 120 people there, 30–40 per cent adults/over 24s, the others were between 12 and 20. We then put two more in place, same theory, worship being constructed by the parishes, advertising and organization by myself and a couple of people from the deanery. We got 107 in Oakham, then 145 in Uppingham. Completely different models – Oakham quite reflective, we used water and candles, a mixture of modern music and Taizé. In Uppingham they did a sin burning. All, in one sense, the hymn-prayer sandwich and a key speaker. The figures have gone up and up – we were averaging 130/140 at all of these. We were getting young people between 12 and 18 plus a number between 20 and 30 who were worshipping in regular congregations but wanted something different. There were then a number of the older people of 40 to 50 and above who wanted a change, wanted something different. They wanted a more lively style of worship and wanted to see young people worshipping.

My sadness is that most of these young people are not being fully engaged on a week-by-week Sunday basis. *Let RYP* has provided an outlet for them but I also fear it has provided an easy way of pushing youth worship into one Sunday a month and the deanery can say, 'They can go to *Let RYP*', or a parish can say, 'We are engaged in youth work, we run a *Let RYP* once a year.'

So *RYP* has become popular; my concern is that young people have, through the success of it, been marginalized again. How to bring them back into Sunday worship is very difficult because they face the same problems – predominately older congregations, clergy in their late 50s. By patting ourselves on the back and saying *RYP* is good we've lost the track of it a bit. We had hoped it would bring about people wanting to engage with young people in services. I do think they want to but I don't think we have the wherewithal to do that.

We imposed it on them – it shouldn't have worked – but it does work in this setting. Because young people don't meet together in groups we have plugged this as a youth group – not that they could have set it up for themselves – because they don't meet together.

From having absolutely nothing, Rutland has a viable youth pro-gramme standing on its own feet, encouraging musicians, encouraging people to consider running youth services in villages and communi-ties that would never have done so. These are just steps that I was told could not happen. In that sense it is great but how you actually get young people worshipping on a Sunday in high participation, I don't know.

Revd Sue Pinnington, formerly in Peterborough Diocese.

Opening up the structures

There are many signs of hope, though we need to take seriously the issue raised earlier of setting up parallel structures which, when successful can marginalize those you wish to bring in. One of the 'growth areas' in the Church is the various forms of youth forums or synods, with talk of a national youth synod. There are those who challenge this approach and in some dioceses there has been a decision not to have a youth synod, but to tackle the issue in other ways. Those who are walking the youth synod path speak with great enthusiasm.

> I jumped at the chance of getting involved because it was a good place where I could get my views heard and we could debate what was going on in diocesan synod. I feel I've been given a chance to have my say about what is going on. I'm just a normal young person where the youth population of our church is me and my brother, so it's good to meet with other young Christians with the same problems and same hopes but also those who have other views but recognize we have common goals and purpose.
>
> Ronan Wade, Loddon, Norfolk.

It is not without its problems, one being how to communicate to the whole Church what youth synod is meant to be.

> I should attend deanery synod, but it seems they don't know what we are for or what we do. Katie has been, and spoke to them, but they still don't seem to be clear about what part we have. Even my PCC don't seem to understand.
>
> Stephanie Rawlings, Heacham, Norfolk.

One of the issues raised by a member of Norwich Youth Synod is, 'Whose agenda?' He challenges whether the youth synod should be debating the same issues as diocesan and General Synod, or facing other issues that he sees as currently more significant.

If I was in diocesan synod I wouldn't have listened to us about marriage – because we've never been there. Everyone was coming out with these views and I was laughing inside myself as none of us are qualified to comment.

I think we should be discussing things like 'youth in the Church, a dying breed'. We should be concentrating on changing that – even the young people in the church are a bit funny about it. We know that kids my age aren't going to things that are boring and tedious. Church – it shouldn't be just fun, but if someone starts going for the 'wrong' reasons they might end up catching the 'right' reasons.

Paul Fawcett, Langham, Norfolk.

A key factor growth area for those involved has been in their own spiritual walk.

Funny thing is I've been brought closer to Christ through this, supported me through a lot of things and grown in my faith. I know that my views are taken into account. You feel valued as well, and what you do.

Stephanie Rawlings, Heacham, Norfolk.

Youth synod has got me believing. I had too many doubts to say I was a true believer. If it hadn't been for synod I wouldn't be a believer now. It was at *Time of Our Lives* that I first started believing – at St Paul's Cathedral – the emotion, the atmosphere was electrifying. If they can get this emotional there must be something in it.

Paul Fawcett, Langham, Norfolk.

No one is saying establishing a youth synod is easy, but there is a real sense of purpose in the people we talked with, and solid hopes for the future.

I'd like to see more participation and more understanding of what youth synod is with all places for youth synod being taken up, with a waiting list of people to have a say. I'd like to know that what youth synod is talking about is being acknowledged, and be part of what the Church is with youth synod as a strong body capable of looking after itself.

Ronan Wade, Loddon, Norfolk.

One of the values of youth synod is that the young people see other people in a similar position as them; they don't feel so much on their own.

I think it has changed attitudes towards young people – no longer taking it for granted that young people want this or that, they now ask – they want to know – the word is spreading.

There is now a group ready to speak and synod are ready to listen.

Katie Knowles, Diocese of Norwich.

Needing support – avoiding tokenism

In the earlier book of this series, *Accompanying*, the focus was upon walking alongside, listening to and supporting people on their journey. It seems an appropriate reminder from the experience of some who have shared their stories that structures cannot just be created or changed, they involve people and they need real support.

Within my home church, the PCC decided to positively 'recruit' young people to stand and two such people were found and elected. When one of these had to stand down the following year for personal reasons, one place on the PCC was advertised for a young person and two stood! As no one wanted an election the second candidate was co-opted – good for youth representation, but what for democracy? However, things did not turn out as hoped.

In raising questions about church decisions I was often referred to the young people on the PCC who were apparently my representatives! Young PCC members do not exclusively represent the youth of a parish – all PCC members should do this, just as the younger people should consider all ages. The communications and articles which I wrote on church policy also caused the young PCC members duress as they were 'picked on' to explain my words. With all this, one of the recently elected young people (and a close friend of mine) resigned. On a personal level she had found the priorities to be misplaced, many issues to be irrelevant, and a lack of discussion and involvement by many. However, her letter of resignation simply stated that she wished to visit different churches and so did not feel able to continue to represent on the PCC. This caused many problems, inappropriate handling of situations, and various repercussions.

From this experience I want to stress the importance that it is not simply a question of getting young people into structures, but once they are there they need great support from inside and outside their church. Structures and people need to be willing to offer this support, and be open to change and innovation rather than dismissing it or simply continuing as before.

Stephen Palmer, Young Adult Network.

This story highlights the difference between participation and tokenism. In a desire to do, and be seen to do the 'right' things we can easily find ourselves falling into the trap of tokenism. As an outcome, something we can measure, it is good for a parish council to have a young person in membership. To involve someone in a church committee means a major commitment by the individual and by the whole committee to enable that person to participate on equal terms, time being given to think through what they want to say; in many ways mirroring what obviously goes on in a youth synod.

In a desire to give young people the freedom to organize and run their own youth worship event a meeting was set up involving the priests and young people. At the second meeting the priests decided to back off and leave the young people to themselves, believing that this would enable them to proceed 'unhindered' by the adult input and influence. Whilst not attending the meetings, they did notice that the number of young people attending the planning meetings was falling. On investigation it turned out that the whole thing, lock, stock, and barrel, had been hijacked by one young woman who was out to get her own way. This highlights the importance of giving appropriate support. Once the priests had left there was no one to challenge the dominant individual. The resulting event reflected one person's ideas and the work with the young people was further back than when they had started out originally. The fear was that the resulting event would reflect only one person's ideas, and the work with the young people would be further back than when we started. Despite all this, and against the 'expert knowledge' of the adult leadership, the other young people came through, challenged the dominant young person and, as a result, an incredible event attracted a wide range of young people who were enabled in the worshipping of God. We have to learn to trust the young people.

Paul Niemiec, Diocesan Youth Officer for Peterborough.

Ecumenical dimension

It is easy to think that we are the only ones engaging in this type of consideration. As we look to our various ecumenical contacts we find the issue of participation is on their agenda as well. Providing opportunities to take responsibility, with appropriate support, enables people to develop their gifts and their self-esteem.

I was asked if I would like to help run a mixed-age afternoon activity at Canterbury Summer Gathering 1999. At first I was a little unsure as I can be quite shy, but I decided that it would be a good experience. It also gave me responsibility at this week-long event where so many people were involved – over 800.

During the (planning) weekend we carefully planned what we would do and even wrote scripts to ensure that we explained activities clearly. We practised activities and explained them in turn. We took different responsibilities and after the weekend I felt much more confident about my role.

When it came to the actual event, I was a little nervous at first but all the careful planning, along with the support of three co-facilitators, made it much easier. It was a challenge with such a broad age range to get everyone comfortable and working together – 5 years old to over 80!

Overall I enjoyed the experience and found it very rewarding, and I am sure that the others did too. The participants seemed to be pleased to see young people getting involved in such a responsible way and I think that everyone enjoyed the activities.

Feedback from participants:

- Seeing a young adult from my meeting leading this session in a self-possessed, confident and charming way! (40ish woman).

- They had obviously spent a long time preparing and giving a good deal of thought to their own presentation techniques as well as content and activities. The three younger members of the team were impressively prepared and organized but still managed to be spontaneous. They were approachable and patient. It was a delight to be in their group. (50-year-old).

- These three young people took their duties very seriously – worked well together, spoke clearly and were efficient in their jobs. (In my 80th year).

- I think it is a good idea that young people have a chance to organize things. (9-year-old).

Angela Gough, aged 17, Quaker Home Service.

In other parts of the Church young people are being taken more seriously and ways are being created for their voice to be more easily heard within the structures. The United Reformed Church has a youth forum which runs alongside its main decision-making body and is allowed to influence it. The Methodist Association of Youth Clubs (MAYC) has produced *Charter* 95 (1995), a document from the young people of the Methodist Church to the leaders.

In 1994 the young people of the Methodist Church did some consulting, which led to the launch of *Charter 95* – a document to help the Church become more inclusive and God-centred. It was aimed at moving the Church forward. This was then passed at the Methodist Conference in Bristol during 1995 and has therefore become part of the Church's focus and work. This has seen new worship resources and a *Risk Kit* develop, as well as the creation of an annual youth conference and the Methodist Youth Executive. These give the youth a way of their own to feed into the Church as a whole. This was the vision of young people for the future of the Church – and is still being developed.

Lucas Meagor, MAYC.

Young Adult Network

In the Church of England we have seen the development of the Young Adult Network (YAN) which grew out of a Young Adult Forum and the Young Adult Observers group at General Synod. Since 1993 when a working group was formed to develop a vision statement and aims, YAN has become an important vehicle for the voice of young adults. In 1996 YAN took a significant role in consultation around and presentation to General Synod of *Youth A Part*. A year later, as a result of the challenges of *Youth A Part*, a member of YAN Executive was co-opted onto the Voluntary and Continuing Education Committee of the Board of Education.

Vision

The Young Adult Network has developed and refined its vision over a long period of time. There has always been an acknowledgement that we needed a strong vision that would focus what we are about and would be the driving force behind our work. In this we have developed a Vision Statement, a key text of scripture which has constantly challenged and inspired us and five key aims which further focus our activity.

Vision statement

We have a vision of a Church in which young adults are consulted, where they are enabled to participate in every level of decision-making and in which their gifts of leadership and innovation are recognized and used.

Key text

I am young in years and you are old; that is why I was fearful, not daring to tell you what I know. I thought, 'Age should speak; advanced years should teach wisdom.' But it is the spirit in mortals, the breath of the Almighty, that gives them understanding. It is not only the old who are wise, not only the aged who understand what is right.

Job 32.6-9 (NIV).

Key aims

1. To challenge young adults to consider their role and involvement within the decision-making structures of the Church.

2. To challenge the whole Church to recognize and use the gifts of leadership and innovation that God has given to many young adults.

3. To challenge those already involved in the synodical structures to be more proactive in their efforts to involve young adults.

4. To see more young people elected to PCCs, deanery synods, diocesan synods and the General Synod in both the short and long term.

5. To pray for, equip and resource those young adults involved within the structures.

In the preparation for this book we invited the Young Adult Network to respond to a number of questions and we encourage you to read the full submission (Appendix 1). One question was to identify factors that work against participation. In this response an important area is highlighted (page 72):

It is without a doubt that the Churches' decision-making bodies are heavily weighted with white middle-class people and in many cases predominantly men. Though many more women are involved than in previous years, we still need to spend more effort involving women, ethnic minority groups and young adults in the way we make decisions.

The Council for Minority Ethnic Concerns (CMEAC) is working to raise awareness of what are undoubtably marginalized groups within the Church of England. We have looked at the real difficulties that exist for young people wishing to participate in the life of the Church. Through the work of the CMEAC, and its recent report *Simply Value Us*, we have to recognize the double marginalization that exists for young people who are of an ethnic minority background. The Stephen Lawrence case and all that has followed highlight the real fears and prejudice that face non-white people in this country. As the Church we cannot ignore this challenge, and whilst we do not attempt to look at it in any depth within *Taking A Part*, we wish to underline the need to seriously address these issues. If as a majority white, middle-class church we struggle to relate with and enable white, middle-class young people, how much more must be done to work with young people from other cultures and communities?

We entitled this chapter 'Risking change' and we are aware that for many of us it can feel like stepping into the dark. However, as the examples throughout this book illustrate, there is work going on, ground being broken. It is therefore about taking a calculated risk where others are already showing us the way. It is often young people who are taking risks, young people who are challenging us to listen as they show us they want to be part of the Church. Young people are asking us to be open to their participation – how will we, the adult Church, respond?

6

What next?

In this book, and in churches all over the country, there are many positive stories of young people being actively involved in their communities and churches. But this is a partial picture and there is no room for self-congratulation or complacency. Remember the story in the introduction of the young people at General Synod with their grim papier mâché masks, foot on the head, hand over the eyes, fist in the mouth – and it is these people who are committed enough to come to the church. Many more young Christians have experienced the Church becoming cold and foreign as they have grown older. Many young people outside the Church walk past church buildings every day with no glimmer of recognition or belonging – still less any understanding of the Christian story.

The question now is how we use the stories and experience of young people, the voices which are in this book, and together work out an inclusive way forward. 'How can I use some of the thoughts gathered in this book in my own church and community?'

Returning to the parable there are some key themes which we might use.

The first is that the master had an understanding of the ability of the servants. He knew them and knew how much money each of them would be able to handle. Often with young people we tend to group them all together without appreciating that they are different, and each has different capacities and skills. The 'Accompanying' model described in the first book of this series shows how we as adults may get alongside young people so that they do not appear as threatening aliens but as people.

The second theme is that when the master returned the two servants who had done well were amply rewarded. Their reward was to share in the master's happiness. The happiness stemmed from the fact that the servants had succeeded – they took on their task and both achieved. The reward for both was the same in spite of one servant having more responsibility, having been entrusted with more money. They were also promised new and extra responsibilities and trust. This gives us an indication of the developmental nature of participation. When people are able to achieve small tasks or responsibilities we rejoice with them and take this as an indication that they are ready for greater things. Too often with young people they are thrust into the deep end, for example, by being given a reading to do in church when they are not prepared or supported and, consequently, they fail embarrassingly. The sad thing is that those who entrusted the job to the young person may decide not to 'risk it' in future, so would choose a 'safe' adult to read rather than prepare and support the young person so they may succeed. Preparation in a learning church can start before children talk, when they may help with gathering the hymn books or with other jobs. This can then be built on so that there is a natural development, and as children acquire greater skills and confidence they can make an increasing range of contributions to the Church and community.

The third theme is centred on the servant who buried his talent out of fear of the master. When *Youth A Part*, the report on young people and the Church, was travelling around the country in the pre-publication consultation, there were two words which we were hearing from all parts of England. These words were 'fear' and 'guilt'. Young people get a bad press from the media – the only things that are reported are when young people are bad or sad. It is not surprising that the older members of the Church can be intimidated and worried about 'the problem of young people'. The fear of the servant stopped him from using his talent, and allowing it to grow and multiply. It is important that we find ways of overcoming our own fear of young people, of the unknown, and can take the risk of using the talent of young people wisely for the whole Church and community.

The fourth theme is that when the servant did not use the talent given to him he was left grinding his teeth and crying. There are many in the Church who are already lamenting about the large number of young people leaving the Church.

In one northern archdeaconry a worker did some research and discovered that 98 per cent of children attending church up to the age of 12 'disappear' from their churches by the time they are 15. Not only is there pain coming from those of us still attached to the Church, but those young people who leave the Church often do it with sadness and a sense of failure.

We need to understand and know our young people, share and rejoice together and develop skills and faith together. We need to work out ways of breaking down the fear barriers, the stereotypes and things that keep young and old apart. We need to take this whole subject seriously, rather than pretending that it might get better by itself.

How can we change our situations so that they are more open to young people's participation? Firstly, we need to know what the situation is now. Secondly, we need to know what we are hoping will happen, to develop an expectation. Thirdly, we need to know when we have succeeded?

One of the key elements in making all of this successful is by starting with young people. Many churches say 'we don't have any young people' but this may overlook the few young people that are there – or the older 'children' just moving into adolescence who could respond to an invitation to be really involved in the church. It is also possible to overlook young people whom we know but who are not 'regular attenders'. A diocesan youth officer in a rural diocese was saying that some young people in his diocese would class themselves as 'regular attenders' if they went to church six times a year. If they were at a rural church where the vicar took services on a rotational basis he or she might only see the young person once or maybe twice a year. Thus the vicar thinks that there are 'no young people' and the young people think that they are 'regular attenders'. The same diocesan youth officer said that if an older member of the congregation failed to turn up to services someone would go and ask if everything was all right. If it is a young person, he said, there is an expectation that this was just 'part of growing up' and they would not be visited. It was also interesting that when the Archbishops offered invitations to 16- to 25-year-olds to attend the *Time of Our Lives* celebration in 1999 a number of 'hidden' young people appeared and have subsequently taken on key roles in their parishes and dioceses.

Perhaps we are being called to 'cast our nets on the other side' and look creatively at the way we can approach and meet young people so that good working and worshipping relationships can be made. If we can do the flip in perception where we see young people as co-workers and, like the adults, a resource for the Church, we will understand our need for them to be involved. We will work hard to make sure that they can contribute to the whole life of the Church by making our structures clearer and more accessible and going the 'extra mile' in order to avail the wider Church and community of their contributions.

When we attempt any change it is much more hopeful if we can see that progress is being made. If we have particular goals and benchmarks which we celebrate as we pass them, it is a much more encouraging process. These goals can help us register the quality of the relationships developing and they can register the quantity of activity which follows this sort of commitment – individual goals, such as for older and younger people in the congregation to spend time with each other or be involved in a specific project; or structural goals such as 'having two young people on the parish council by next year'. It is important to start small, learn through the successes and failures and build up the energy and impetus. As we said earlier, when young people realize that they are not seen simply as empty containers to be filled up, but that the wider Church really wants and needs their contributions, there can be real energy and transformation. Other indications that young people are involved are when they are 'at home' with church structures, when older church members realize better decisions are being made with young people's input, or when events and church committees, etc., work round young people's key commitments. There are many ways of measuring whether the culture in our own church or community is becoming more young people 'friendly' and accessible.

However we decide to encourage participation in our own situations, the most important thing is that we start now. In writing this book we hope we have gathered ways of thinking about participation, models of analysis we can use, stories which can inspire our own work. It has been a privilege to hear what good work is going on, and to be in touch with the enthusiasm and ability of young people in our churches. There are more stories than we could hope to contain here, and many are still being 'written'. They may speak of new vision of what can be changed, they may speak of what has happened. Some will be good news, some will share the mistakes, but we believe in the power of stories and the need to tell each other for encouragement and to show what is possible. Our hope is that the ideas and thoughts in the book will inspire people to confront fears and for both young and old to work, worship and develop together.

Appendix 1

Submission from the Young Adult Network

Introduction

In this paper we have tried to address the questions put to us:

- What does Young Adult Network hope to achieve?

- What is your vision – the place where you want to be?

- How are you getting there – your planning and methods?

- How do you think the Church will change as a result of the Young Adult Network?

- Can you identify what things block young adult participation?

- Can you identify what releases these blocks?

- Can you trace the history of Young Adult Network?

Section One deals with participation issues, what blocks there are and how we address them. Section Two deals with the questions directly regarding the Network.

Section One

In order for us to fully understand how and why young adults should be involved at every level of decision-making in the Church of England, we must first look at the nature of the Church and how it works. These same factors will also help us to understand why so often the systems we use actually work against the involvement of young adults. In this section we will not only look at the Church but briefly look at the ways in which young people are excluded and highlight some of the strategies we can develop to address this.

The Church

The nature and authority of the Church

To understand the way the Church is governed we must first understand its nature:

● The Church of England is just one part of the whole Church of God; holy, catholic and apostolic.

● Authority in the Church is taken from God as creator, redeemer and sustainer of the world.

All members of the Church have a responsibility for its life and witness. It follows that there are appropriate ways in which everyone shares in the process by which the life of the Church is fashioned and its mission resourced.

Christ has given authority to the Church. He has also given gifts through the Holy Spirit, such as leadership, teaching and pastoral care that the people of God might be equipped for their ministry and spiritual life (John 20.21-23; Matthew 28.18-20; Ephesians 4.7-16).

So each of us, as Christians and in this instance Anglicans too, has a responsibility for each other within the Body of Christ. We exercise this by caring for each other pastorally and in holding each other to account.

Led by bishops and governed by synods – The role of synod in the Church of England

The Church attempts to combine leadership by bishops (bishops exercise that role in relation to their priests, deacons and the lay people in their diocese as well as with their brother bishops) with government of the Church by synods which include representative clergy and laity. This inevitably involves holding different forms of authority in tension. At the end of the day the authority of the bishops and the authority of the synods have to be held in creative tension, the bishop leading in consultation and discussion with representative clergy and laity.

The term 'synod' has its origin in two Greek words, *sun* meaning 'together' and *hodos* meaning 'the way', and was commonly used in

Greek communities to describe their own system of assembling qualified citizens in order to discover the common will.

The Church of England believes it important to include all its members in the understanding of Christian truth and in the government of the Church. Synodical government is an attempt to seek and find the mind of Christ for his Church, as well as consensus in the ordering of the Church's life. The particular form of government reflects the history of the Church as well as the theological principle.

So the way we make decisions is important as it models collegiality and partnership. The 'synods' are designed to bring together the community of God to discern God's will. By missing out some elements of that community the decision-making process is not only undermined but the 'body' does not function quite as it should or ought.

All are called

So God has given both authority and gifts to his people the Church and sustains them by the power of the Holy Spirit. God continues to give all the Church needs for its mission and leadership (the theology of the gracious gift as expressed in the Turnbull report (*Working as One Body*, 1.10, p. 4). Each of us has a vital part to play in the life, work, mission and ministry of his Church (I Corinthians 12.12-26). We are called to participate in the life of the Church and God equips us for that service.

This calling is not just about ordained ministers but for each one of us regardless of our age. Everyone has something to offer for the enrichment of the Body of Christ, the Church. Calling is about the whole people of God (the *laos* where we get laity from) living as disciples – recognizing their called status and the gifts they have been given and using those gifts in the ministry and mission of the Church.

God gives each one of us gifts. Each one of us has a unique role to play in the life of the Church and in some way the Church is diminished if 'each part of the body does not play its part'. The Church and its leadership have an important role in enabling each person to play their part.

Factors that work against participation

As with so many areas there is not one, single concern that can be pinpointed and worked on to resolve the issue of participation. There are many factors, which combine to impede that inclusion. Below some of those factors are highlighted:

- The structures can and often do seem remote to the rest of the Church's life and particularly to its active mission and ministry. There is a sense that the structures do not engage in 'real' or ordinary issues.

- Many elements of the decision-making processes are informed through the written word and are often weighty documents filled with acronyms and jargon. This can be most unhelpful to some, especially those who are not academic, though not exclusively so!

- There is a tendency for individuals to hold on to power especially if there is not a rotational system in place for elections.

- In many places there is a perception that you need a great deal of experience before you can become involved in decision-making and that young people either don't have gifts that can be useful in that context or that their gifts are best used elsewhere.

- Students find it particularly difficult to become involved because they spend half their year in one parish and diocese and often the other half in a completely different parish and diocese.

- There is an age barrier to some elements of the structures (e.g. to be elected to diocesan synod and General Synod you have to be eighteen).

- There is an attitude that says we deliver things to young people. Youth work is seen as being delivered by adults to young people, rather than a partnership where adults and young people work together. The perception is given of a lesser status for young people when it is often not intended.

- It is without a doubt that the Church's decision-making bodies are heavily weighted with white middle class people and in many cases predominantly men. Though many more women are involved than in previous years we still need to spend more effort involving women, ethnic minority groups and young adults in the way we make decisions.

- Often meetings of committees or bodies such as the General Synod are held during the week when many are at work or college and cannot easily take time off.

Strategies for change

Such multi-faceted issues cannot be solved by a single neat solution but demand a variety of responses to suit the situation:

- Training and skills development should be available for all those who join the decision-making structures whether they are young or older. Such training could be organized by dioceses and led by experienced trainers and those who have developed skills and experience from their involvement. The training should be free, sensitive to cultural and education needs and be practical in nature.

- The rules the Church has set to order the decision-making structures (Church Representation Rules and the Standing Orders) should be carefully analysed in consultation with those groups who are under-represented, to highlight areas for concern and begin to address them.

- Promote and share aspects of the Church's rules that allow flexibility and profile good examples of this such as PCCs with young people under sixteen as observers.

- We need to promote and highlight innovation and good practice in projects and work that develop a positive ethos in youth work and work that breaks down differences, stereotypes. Work that brings different generations together should also be profiled in this way.

- Promote opportunities for young people and young adults to have a voice in the structures, such as youth PCCs, young people's consultation or focus groups, youth forums and diocesan youth synods.

- Promote more reflection about the nature of the Church, the discovery and use of gifts, and further produce materials that help individuals and groups develop and apply those skills.

- Cultivate a better understanding about the decision-making structures and what they are about and do. Primarily this is a communication exercise to share information in a relevant way.

These are just a fraction of the things the Church could develop to begin the process of changing attitudes, opening up the structures and empowering people to make a contribution. What is important is that work is carried out in partnership, strategically and with a balance being given to the short, medium and long term goals.

Section Two

Vision

The Young Adult Network has developed and refined its vision over a long period of time. There has always been an acknowledgement that we needed a strong vision that would focus what we are about and would be the driving force behind our work. In this we have developed a Vision Statement, a key text of scripture which has constantly challenged and inspired us and five key aims which further focus our activity.

Vision statement

We have a vision of a Church in which young adults are consulted, where they are enabled to participate in every level of decision-making and in which their gifts of leadership and innovation are recognized and used.

Key text

> I am young in years and you are old; that is why I was fearful, not daring to tell you what I know. I thought, 'Age should speak; advanced years should teach wisdom.' But it is the spirit in mortals, the breath of the Almighty, that gives them understanding. It is not only the old who are wise, not only the aged who understand what is right.
>
> Job 32.6-9 (NIV)

Key aims

- To challenge young adults to consider their role and involvement within the decision-making structures of the Church.

- To challenge the whole Church to recognize and use the gifts of leadership and innovation that God has given to many young adults.

- To challenge those already involved in the synodical structures to be more proactive in their efforts to involve young adults.

- To see more young people elected to PCCs, deanery synods, diocesan synods and the General Synod in both the short and long term.

- To pray for, equip and resource those young adults involved within the structures.

Network structure

The current structure comprises a Working Group with young adults drawn from various dioceses many of whom have attended General Synod as observers. They are responsible for policy and overall management of the Network.

In turn the executive officers act on behalf of the Working Group in managing the Network's activities.

Both groups work in partnership with the National Youth Office of the Board of Education of the Archbishops' Council of the Church of England.

Achieving our aims

As the Network has developed we have become more focused on our Key Aims and the need to think strategically if we were to work within our resources. We published a Strategy Document for 1998, 1999 and 2000. This helped us to focus our attention on activities we felt would be beneficial over the short, medium and long term. Below are the five key aims along with work we have undertaken, are currently engaged in or are planning for the immediate future.

To challenge young adults to consider their role and involvement within the decision-making structures of the Church:

- Currently we do this mainly through working with individual dioceses.

- The Young Adult Observer Group has been a useful opportunity for young adults interested in the structures to 'taste and see' what General Synod is like. It has proved a valuable opportunity for them to explore what area if any they want to get more involved in.

- This year we will launch a newsletter – *MAGNET* – to stimulate interest in participation issues and support those involved as well as to share information and good practice.

- We will also be broadening the Working Group's scope to be more of a network rooted in the diocese that will engage more meaningfully on a more local setting.

To challenge the whole Church to recognize and use the gifts of leadership and innovation that God has given to many young adults:

- Currently we are working on an opportunity to bring young adults, diocesan youth officers and others together to explore ways in which young adults can meaningfully engage in the structures and highlight areas that need change. We hope this will form the basis of a General Synod Miscellaneous Paper.

- We are beginning work on resources that will help the Church to recognize the gifts each one of us has to offer through materials on using our gifts and methods of discovering our own gifts.

- In the near future we want to develop 'Enablers' – people who may or may not be on PCCs – who want to encourage young adults in their parish to share and participate in all aspects of the parish's life but in particular decision-making through the PCC. They would act as accompanists to the young adult, providing support and encouragement on the journey.

To challenge those already involved in the synodical structures to be more proactive in their efforts to involve young adults:

- The Network has developed a number of relationships with members of the General Synod and the Archbishops' Council in order to promote the work of the Network and the need to encourage participation.

- The Young Adult Observer Group has built up a reputation amongst members of General Synod. The observers have done this through engaging with members socially, through contribution to some debates, the receptions held each year and by leading worship.

- The Network is planning to support any young adult who stands for election to the General Synod from any diocese. We are engaging the help of General Synod members in this process (i.e. helping draft election addresses, help with strategy).

- We hope the GS Misc. Paper will once again influence the General Synod to reflect on the need for young adult participation and the need to develop creative and innovative strategies to promote this.

To see more young people elected to PCCs, deanery synods, diocesan synods and the General Synod in both the short and long term:

- We will be writing to each parish in order to promote young adult participation, the work of the Network and *PCCs Uncovered*. We hope this will provide opportunities for parishes to reflect on participation and how they might respond.

- The Network is planning to support any young adult who stands for election to the General Synod from any diocese. We are engaging the help of General Synod members in this process (i.e. helping draft election addresses, help with strategy).

- The Network uses its extensive contacts to promote young adult participation in an attempt constantly to reiterate the need for young adult participation. In doing so and by providing opportunities for young adults to engage with decision-makers we hope to influence attitudes both in the short and long term.

- We are seeking to develop greater contacts with those dioceses that have set up or are creating diocesan youth synods, forums and councils. We hope to be able to learn from them and develop links between them and the Network.

To pray for, equip and resource those young adults involved within the structures:

- We hope that *MAGNET*, our new newsletter, will be a platform to promote more prayerful support for young adults, especially peer support.

- The report *Accompanying* has and continues to promote the principle of supporting young adults in their spiritual journey through 'mentors' and other models such as 'prayer triplets' and 'study groups'.

- Publishing *PCCs Uncovered*, a resource aimed at young adults serving on PCCs or thinking about it. This has been a major project for the Network and is the fruit of much hard work. We have learned a great deal from the process. We hope it will be the first of many practical and widely used resources.

- We would hope that the 'Enablers' initiative would also help to provide pastoral support to young adults who are involved in or considering any such involvement in the structures.

Ecumenical work

- We have always paid great attention to the need to develop effective relationships with our ecumenical partners. We were founding partners of the Joint Churches Youth Service Initiative, *Youth Forum*, which brought together representatives from the seven major denominations. This is now the CTE Youth Forum (Churches Together in England Youth Forum) which has the potential of bringing young adults from the 22 member Churches together to promote an understanding of each other, share information and resources and promote unity in our diversity.

Changes in the Church as a result of our work

Ultimately the Network and its activities seek to fulfil our purpose in bringing about a Church in which young adults are consulted, where they are enabled to participate in every level of decision-making and in which their gifts of leadership and innovation are recognized and used, which is our vision and the focus of our work.

There are many levels to our work, some of which is measurable and much which isn't, certainly in the short term at least. We are in the business of influencing change and attitudes, none of which change overnight and certainly not when it is within the context of an institution like the Church of England. Some would say the Network has worked within the systems of the Church of England too rigidly and that we have consulted too widely about too many things and this has impeded our growth.

Obviously we cannot bring this about on our own; we work in partnership with the National Youth Office, other national bodies, the diocesan youth officers, diocesan youth synods and councils, youth workers, parishes and young adults themselves! The Network cannot and would not claim exclusively the credit for changes that have happened or are happening. It is a collaboration from many sources that brings about change in our work and attitudes. In saying this I make a presumption that entwined in all this activity is the transforming power of God at work in our lives through the power of the Holy Spirit.

Conclusion

The Network is doing a great deal already, yet it needs to do so much more. It needs to focus on its vision whilst responding to the need to grow, develop and change. In this it needs to:

● reorganize its own structures to be more open and collaborative;

● promote and resource inter-diocesan networking to share information, news, innovative ideas and good practice;

● develop more direct work with young adults to encourage participation and provide the right resources and information that will facilitate that;

● develop and promote new innovative and practical models of consultation and participation for all levels of the structures;

● work with diocesan youth synods and councils.

Appendix 2

General Synod, July 2000: Resolutions

General Synod in York, July 2000, debated *Youth A Part: The Facts and the Future* (GS 1381), a report which detailed the progress following the *Youth A Part* debate in 1996. The following resolutions were carried:

'That the Synod do take note of this Report.'

'That this Synod welcome the positive work resulting from *Youth A Part* and commend those working at National, Diocesan and Parish levels to:

(a) enable young people to make an active contribution to the worship and mission of the Church, especially with regard to evangelism and social justice;

(b) actively encourage young people's participation in decision-making in the Church and to reduce structural and cultural blocks which inhibit this, especially with reference to minority ethnic concerns, and, to this end, request the Bridge Follow-up Group, in consultation with the Young Adult Network, to bring back proposals to enable young people to participate more effectively in Synodical government;

(c) secure resources to enable young people to be active in the Church's mission;

(d) continue to work with the Government and other agencies in responding to the alienation of many young people in society and to endorse the positive contribution of the Youth Service; and

(e) undertake to review further progress in 2005.

Bibliography

Sam Adams, *The Process of Change through Relationships between Adults and Young People*, Paper given at Conference on Youth Ministry, Mansfield College, Oxford, January 1995.

Archbishops' Commission on Rural Areas, *Faith in the Countryside*, Churchman Publishing, 1990.

Board of Education of the General Synod, *Youth A Part*, National Society/Church House Publishing, 1996.

J. Macalister Brew, *In the Service of Youth*, Faber & Faber, 1943.

Sue Cockerill, 'Equality and empowerment: The principles of the youth work curriculum?', *Youth and Policy*, Issue Number 36, March 1992.

Committee for Minority Ethnic Anglican Concerns (CMEAC), *Simply Value Us* (CMEAC Youth Research Project), Church House Publishing, 2000.

John Denham and Martin Notley, *A Democratic Voice? The Changing Role of Youth Councils*, National Youth Bureau, 1982.

Paulo Freire, *Pedagogy of the Oppressed*, Penguin, 1995.

Maxine Green and Chandu Christian, *Accompanying Young People on Their Spiritual Quest*, National Society/Church House Publishing, 1998.

Charles Handy, *The Empty Raincoat*, Arrow Business Books, 1995.

Diarmuid Kearney and Eamonn Keenan, 'Empowerment: Does anyone know what it means?', *Journal of the Extern Organization*, Lynx, SPCK, 1988.

Frank Lake, *Clinical Theology*, Yeomans, Darton, Longman and Todd, 1986.

Methodist Association of Youth Clubs Manchester and Stockport District, *Is Charter 95 Consistent With Other Research?*, MAYC, 1995.

Dave Phillips and Alison Skinner, *Nothing Ever Happens Around Here: Developing Work with Young People in Rural Areas*, Youth Work Press, 1994.

Jacqui Schiff et al., *The Cathexis Reader*, Harper and Row, 1975.

Gillian Stamp, *Stealing the Churches' Clothes?*, Brunel Institute of Organization and Social Studies, Brunel University, 1992.

Gillian Stamp, *The Enhancement of Ministry in Uncertainty*, Brunel Institute of Organization and Social Studies, Brunel University,1993.

Ian Stewart and Vann Joines, TA *Today*, Lifespace Publishing, 1987.

Alan Thompson, *Experience and Participation, Report of the Review Group on the Youth Service in England*, HMSO, 1982.

Rob White, 'Social Justice, Skill Formation and Australian Youth Work Practice', in *Youth and Policy*, Issue Number 30, June 1990.

Working as One Body: The Report of the Archbishops' Commission on the Organisation of the Church of England, Church House Publishing, 1995.

David H. Wright, *Co-operatives and Community: The Theory and Practice of Producer Co-operatives*, Bedford Square Press of the National Council of Social Service, 1979.